Toward actualizing
human potential

Other books by Robert Carkhuff available from Human Resource Development Press:

Art of Helping IV
Skills of Helping
Art of Program Development
Art of Problem Solving
Art of Developing a Career—Helper's Guide
Teaching as a Treatment
Skills of Teaching—Content Development Skills
Skills of Teaching—Lesson Planning Skills
Skills of Teaching—Interpersonal Skills
Skills of Teaching—Teaching Delivery Skills
The Skilled Teacher—A Systems Approach to Teaching Skills

TOWARD ACTUALIZING HUMAN POTENTIAL

Robert R. Carkhuff

Human Resource Development Press

HUMAN RESOURCE DEVELOPMENT PRESS

Human
Resource
Development
Press

Copyright © 1981 by Human Resource Development Press, 22 Amherst Rd., Amherst, Massachusetts 01002. (413) 253-3488. All rights reserved. No part of the material protected by this copyright notice may be reproduced or utilized in any form or by any means, electronic or mechanical, including photocopy, recording, or by any information storage and retrieval system, without permission from the copyright owner.

ISBN Number 0-914234-15-3
Library of Congress Catalogue Number 80-84884

First Printing

Manufactured in the United States of America

About the author

In the spring of 1979, Robert R. Carkhuff conducted an international tour during which he gave keynote addresses and led training sessions at a number of institutions in Italy, Brazil, and Venezuela. This text is based on those addresses, all of which converge upon the theme of "Actualizing Human Potential."

Carkhuff is one of the one hundred most-cited social scientists of our time, along with such historical figures as Freud, Marx, and Dewey. He is best known as the author of three of the one hundred most-cited works in the social sciences—*Toward Effective Counseling and Psychotherapy* and two volumes on *Helping and Human Relations*. In addition, he has authored the path-finding text on *The Development of Human Resources* and the *Art of Helping* and *Skills of Teaching* series.

Contents

I
Introduction

1
$E = mc^2$

In his second relativity paper, Einstein made a historic deduction: If a body gives off an amount of energy (E) in the form of light, its mass will be reduced by that amount divided by the speed of light squared ($M = E/c^2$). He then made a great intellectual leap in transforming the algebraic equation: $E = mc^2$.

This new formula established that even a small amount of matter held the power of tons of explosives. This opened the door to the nuclear age. It also led to an explanation of why the sun could burn for so many billions of years while not shrinking appreciably in size.

Einstein himself said:

It is customary to express the equivalence of mass and energy (though somewhat inexactly) by the formula $E = mc^2$, in which c represents the velocity of light, about 186,000 miles per second. E is the energy that is contained in a stationary body; m is its mass. The energy that belongs to the mass m is equal to this mass, multiplied by the square of the enormous speed of light—which is to say, a vast amount of energy for every unit of mass.

> *But if every gram of material contains this tremendous energy, why did it go so long unnoticed? The answer is simple enough: so long as none of the energy is given off externally, it cannot be observed. It is as though a man who is fabulously rich would never spend or give away a cent; no one could tell how rich he was (Einstein, 1956, pp. 51–52).*

So it is with human beings. All are fabulously rich with potential. Few ever spend or give away a cent.

All human beings have the energy equivalent of tons of explosives—enough to energize not one but many lifetimes—if they will but commit their physical resources.

All human beings have the emotional potential to expand their humanity to incorporate within their boundaries all manner of life throughout the ages—if they will but open to their emotional experience.

All human beings have the intellectual potential to grasp the wisdom of the ages while implementing the vision of the future. They can become what they will be—if they will but choose to use their intellects.

Yes, human beings can become masters of their own destinies, using their most precious gifts to shape or reshape their worlds as well as or, perhaps, better than those into which they were thrust. But to do so they must choose to live fully.

The most precious gift of all is the gift of intelligence. It is this gift that allows us to go places we have never been, to become people we have never known. It is this gift that allows us to throw a skyhook to our visions of what can be—energized by our physical resources, mobilized by our emotional resources, operationalized by our intellectual resources. It is this gift that enables us to pull ourselves to our own ideal in fulfilling our visions of humanity.

No civilization in the history of humankind reached a state of advancement without logic. All decayed when they abandoned the use of logic. Nothing else—no religion or political or economic theory—allows us to describe the conditions of our existence, predict the effects of these conditions, and create or recreate our worlds to achieve desirable effects and avoid the undesirable.

A practical application of this gift has been demonstrated most fully with our success in landing a person on the moon. Pursuing the concept or vision, NASA's Dr. John Houbolt developed the objective of a lunar-orbit rendezvous by separating the lunar-landing mission into precise functions to which were assigned specific spacecraft parts. Thus, he *operationalized* putting a person on the moon—a product of humankind's most vivid imagination.

Anything that can be conceived can be operationalized. It follows that anything that can be operationalized can be achieved. It was purely a mechanical implementation process that launched the spacecraft to fulfill the mission and the vision.

So it is also with the most humbly endowed learner. By analyzing his or her needs in the context toward which he or she will move; by objectifying the outcomes with which we will measure and, thus, recycling and refining our learning programs; by developing our content to a skills objective; by organizing our content around experiential learning; by emphasizing kinesthetic teaching methods; by individualizing atomistic learning programs; by beginning with the learner's frame of reference and making all learning instrumental for the learner's purposes; by doing all of these tasks—and more—we can operationalize the launching of a child to land on the planets of inner or outer space. We can fill him or her up with self and expand boundaries to fulfill a personal mission in the world.

Clearly, humankind's goals in space or on Earth are limited only by the boundaries of our intellect. Hopefully, we will not forego our home on Earth prematurely. Hopefully, we will reach for the stars here on Earth.

To accomplish these wondrous goals—to actualize our human potential—we need make only a slight transformation in Einstein's basic formula of physical energy. If we define the E as our personal energy potential or effectiveness and the m as our motivation or emotional "pull" to become something that we are not and the c to be our competencies to operationalize our goals and technologize our programs to achieve our goals through the use of our intellect, then we can transform Einstein's equation into an equation for actualizing human potential:

$$E \quad = \quad m \quad \cdot \quad c^2$$
(Energy   (motivation) (competencies)
potential)

As can be seen in the formula, the power is in the intellect with the emotional dimension serving as a catalyst to activate the development of competencies. Our energy potential or our ability to actualize our potential is a function of our emotional motivation and our compounded intellectual competencies.

We can use this formula to guide us through the chapters of this book. Later on, we will refine it to a more precise definition that we can use to guide ourselves through the chapters of our lives. The chapters are varied, with each viewing the actualizing of human potential from a unique yet sequential perspective.

The following chapter considers the concepts of human potential as implied or inferred by the major positions concerned with human development and rehabilitation. Most of these positions are philosophical and conceptual. They constitute potential sources from which we may begin to describe the effective ingredients of actualizing human potential.

Chapter three suggests that even in those instances where people have moved towards principles of actualizing—as in Maslow's work—the principles are not operationalized. Without this operationalization, we cannot achieve these dimensions and actualize our potential.

The fourth chapter explores the dimensions of human potential and studies clinically some people who have set about to actualize them. Clearly, while they are distinguished by the uniqueness of their contributions, each of these people share a common core of experience. Perhaps the biblical quote expressed by one of those studied is most appropriate: "Then shall I know even as also I am known."

Chapter five explores the sources of human development and change. The fundamental sources are other humans—in their infinite variety of experiences and behaviors—and the limited sources for communicating them. All of these influencing processes culminate in systematically developed insights and actions that enable people to plan and achieve effectively in their worlds.

The sixth chapter moves toward operationalizing human potential. The dimensions measured here include physical fitness, emotional motivation, interpersonal relations, intellectual substance, learning skills, and teaching skills.

In chapter seven, we describe the data distinguishing self-actualizing people from non-actualizing people: physical stamina, a mission outside oneself, interpersonal initiative, substantive skills, action learning skills, and individualized teaching programs.

The eighth chapter presents case studies of self-actualizing people. They are characterized by their creativity and productivity and perseverance in all dimensions of human potential. Their creativity allows them to operationalize worthwhile human goals and their productivity enables them to technologize the means to achieving the goals. Their perseverance assures that they will continue over a lifetime to be creative and productive in spite of all obstacles and crises.

The ninth chapter details the assumptions and implications for a fully functioning human being. The most fundamental assumption is that life is growth. The most fundamental implication is that the pursuit of growth is worth any price—even death—for we are not alive if we are not growing.

Chapter ten considers human potential in relation to marginality and variability. The underlying principle is that those people who are both most marginal and most variable contribute the most to society by moving society toward relative variability and absolute health.

The eleventh chapter develops a model for actualizing human potential. Succinctly, the function of the actualization process is to grow in the quantity and quality of physical, emotional and intellectual resources.

Chapter twelve describes the learning processes and the learnings of a fully functioning person. They are one and the same—open to input, processed to personalize, focused in output. The essence of actualizing human potential is learning to learn.

Finally, the thirteenth chapter refines the formula for actualizing human potential. For our purposes, an actualized human being is physically fit, emotionally motivated, and intellectually skilled. In full, the actualized human being is no more or less than the product of his or her experiences and imagination, with each in tandem exerting a pull upon the other to catch up.

When we speak or write of actualizing human potential, we are conceptualizing the fulfillment of the possible. A person may be making a thrust in either the physical, emotional, or intellectual areas. The concern is with providing the support base necessary to fulfill the potential in the designated area.

For example, in the physical area, a person may want to actualize his or her potential. The goal may be to increase time and/or distance in running, or it may be to excel in some other athletic endeavor such as hitting a ball or throwing a discus. There are already available scientifically based, computerized, biomedical analyses for approximating the limits of physical output of an individual. Thus, programs can be designed to improve performance and actualize potential in the chosen arena. Most important for the individual is developing that person to a higher level of satisfaction in his or her performance.

In the emotional and interpersonal arenas, the analysis is similar. For example, people may wish to fulfill themselves in special relationships with their spouses, children, friends, or other loved ones. There are systematic ways of projecting the upper limits of satisfaction or fulfillment in both quantitative and qualitative terms. Thus, for example, the number of sensitive and responsive human contacts culminating in individualized courses of action may be analyzed. Emotional and interpersonal goals may be set and programs designed to achieve the goals to the satisfaction of the individual involved.

Similar illustrations also apply in the intellectual arena. For example, most people have only vague concepts of where they want to go and what they want to do with their lives. There are systematic ways of operationalizing the concepts as objectives and developing the steps and supportive knowledge needed to achieve these objectives—any objectives—such as learning skills in a particular content area or designing the objectives of an entire career.

Some people, some very few people—certainly less than one in one hundred and perhaps as few as one in one thousand or ten thousand—are concerned with actualizing their full human potential. To do so means pushing their limits physically, emotionally, and intellectually. The higher the achievements in any one of these areas, the higher the achievements in the remaining areas. There is a "bootstrap effect" of movement: As we move forward in one area we pull upon the other areas. Thus, if we develop our physical energy potential through a fitness program, our fitness will have positive effects on the development of our emotional and intellectual potential. Similarly, if we establish mutually reciprocating warm and responsive interpersonal relationships culminating in personalized initiative for both of the parties, the effects will be positive in the areas of physical and intellectual productivity. Further, if we learn how to learn intellectually, we can apply these skills beneficially in the physical and emotional areas of functioning.

There are some who argue that it is not enough to actualize one's potential physically, emotionally, and intellectually. Or put another way, if we do so, the whole is more than the sum of the parts. Many of these people who argue so are proponents of the principle of "spiritual grace": That is, there is a spiritual grace that accompanies human achievements.

What is the nature of this spiritual potential? Suffice it for now to say that beyond living every moment with energy and vitality, experiencing every situation with intensity and immediacy, and individualizing every course of action to achieve every personalized goal, actualizing spiritual potential means being in harmony and congruency with one's universe.

The human potential that exists within each individual, then, is—like that in physical energy—enormous. It is unknown except perhaps by a relative handful of people throughout the history of the world. Like Einstein's law, the law for actualizing human potential permits us to calculate in advance just how much physical energy will be released, how much emotional intensity will be experienced, and how many intellectual products will be produced.

REFERENCES

Einstein, A. *Out of My Later Years*. Secaucus, N.J.: Citadel Press, 1956.

II
The exploration
of actualizing

2
Some models of human development

In the 1960s and 1970s, I had the privilege of working with the Black and Brown communities in so-called social action programs. It is debatable who learned more—they or I. When we began to work with chronically unemployed and underemployed workers; with kids who were not even old enough to drop out of school; and with parents, teachers, and employers who were scared out of their wits by the potential destructiveness of the kids; we did not know if we could succeed. We scrambled to learn everything that we could so that we could teach these young people everything they needed to know. We also ended up training ourselves out of our jobs because we taught them everything we knew. They took care of the rest. Developmentally, we learned two profound principles: (1) It is never too early to initiate human development programs; (2) It is never too late to initiate human development programs.

It is traditional in academic realms to conceive of human development as a succession of states that the child goes through. As with all conceptional frameworks, the theoretical models go beyond the data that describes movement from infancy to adulthood or beyond to the self-actualization of human resources. In other words, these models carry the excess baggage of theoretical constructs that, while humanistic in value, do not translate necessarily to human benefits. For the most part, while they describe the facts, concepts, and principles of human development, their goals are not operational and, thus, the means to achieve these goals are not available.

In this context, children are compared typically to adults on gross physical, emotional, and intellectual characteristics (Grothberg, 1976) (see Table 2-1). As can be seen, the adult is distinguished from the child by such physical dimensions as size and fitness for living. In addition, emotionally the child is unstable and egocentric, while the adult gains stability and expands to include others in his or her concerns. Finally, the child is illiterate and emotional, while the adult acquires his or her greatest skill, human logic, to become literate and rational.

Other dimensions such as social may be added. For example, along the social dimension the child is essentially amoral and consumptive in orientation, while the adult becomes moral and productive. Further, defining career as the way a person lives his or her life, the child's career choices and development are random and dependent, while the adult's are planned and independent. All of these factors are among the many distinguishing characteristics that have been observed throughout the cultures of humankind.

PHYSICAL DEVELOPMENT

The most explicit descriptors of physiological development are those that depict growth in infants and the very young (see Table 2-2). Beyond these early childhood scales, physical maturation tends to

TABLE 2-1   Dimensions distinguishing children and adults

Dimensions	Children	Adults
Physical	Small and unfit	Large and fit
Emotional	Unstable and egocentric	Stable and sociocentric
Intellectual	Illiterate and emotional	Literate and rational

TABLE 2-2   Infant motor skills sequence

Skill	Approximate age in months
Chin up (can raise chin when prone)	1
Head erect	2
Chest up (can raise chest when prone)	2
Head erect and steady	3
Sits with support	4
Sits alone	6
Crawls	7–9
Creeps	9–11
Walks with help	10–12
Stands alone	11–14
Walks alone	11–15

be reported in conjunction with progress in other competencies such as emotional, interpersonal, or intellectual development. Further, much of what is relevant to physiological development as a whole is closely linked to and can be demonstrated by looking at neurological developments in adults.

There are at least three current lines of neurological research that are relevant to human development (Agazarian, et al., 1972). The first involves modifying autonomic bodily functions through conditioning techniques; the second concerns physiological development as it relates to sensory stimuli; and the third relates to the bodily response to environmental stress conditions. The culmination of these studies results in the creation of a possible model for "physiological actualization."

The first mode of research that concerns the autonomic bodily functions (i.e., those bodily functions that seem to be automatic: lungs, heart, kidney, etc.) is based primarily on animal experiments in conditioning techniques. The experiments indicate that emotional states cause autonomic changes that signal and characterize their presence. Similarly, there is a growing line of evidence that indicates that emotional and intellectual states that are mediated by the brain control and can modify endocrine functions. By using appropriate learning techniques these mechanisms can be measured and modified according to an individual's needs.

Although "bio-feedback" techniques have received premature and cultish exploitation, they have provided important examples of conscious control mechanisms through the measurement of skin temperature, electrical resistance of the skin, muscle tension, heart rate, blood pressure, and even electrical brain waves of specific dimensions. These measuring techniques, used correctly, can provide a basis for individual practice in controlling minor physiological changes.

The second line of neurological research addresses both the deprivation and the overload of sensory stimuli and their effect on a developing individual. Sensory deprivation is characterized by the lack of sensory input, particularly early in life. This deprivation has been seen to have a direct and profound effect upon physical development. In institutional children, sensory deprivation compounded with emotional deprivation has been shown to cause mental impairment and regression. Lifespan, physical coordination, and even cognitive development all seem to be negatively affected by sensory deprivation.

On the other hand research efforts suggest that humans are also detrimentally sensitive to overstimulation. Just as there is a range of temperature that can be tolerated by humans, there appears to be a tolerance band for sensory input. Although there is little hard data about the impact of sensory overload on the physical development of children, the possible relationship of this overload to motivation is beginning to surface.

The third category of research that is pertinent to the understanding of neurological elements that lead to physical development involves measuring physical tolerance levels in extremely stressful environments (i.e., the "zero gravity" of space exploration and the extreme pressure encountered in underwater exploration). The effects of these stressful environmental situations, coupled with the gauging of the normal stress needed by the body, begin to give us a clearer understanding of physiological development.

Flowing from group dynamics research, there is a growing attempt to increase both cognitive and affective awareness of physical functioning as a means of improving the "whole person." Four elements of physical development that may be seen as indicators of the relationship between physical fitness and physical, emotional, and intellectual functioning are (1) the suggestion that the body tends to atrophy without use, (2) the knowledge that exercise provides the necessary resistance required by the body, (3) the gauging of healthy sensory inputs, and (4) the strides made in conscious physiological control. Eventually, existing physical development programs will focus upon fitness training augmented by behavior modification techniques to modify bodily functions and to enhance cognitive control of well-being.

EMOTIONAL DEVELOPMENT

Emotions are complex feeling states that are modified by internal and external experiences. Reports of work being done to analyze the complex components of affect are sparse. Cognition itself is in many important ways inseparable from affect. It can be seen clearly as we progress through the composite of work available on emotional development that as the human body grows within the environment, the internal impulses become shaped and modeled by external demands, until there is a bridge formed between the intellectual and the emotional elements. These elements render the transition from one to the other almost indistinguishable. There are, however, some important distinctions in emotional development that can be made.

Perhaps the natural beginning point for a consideration of the emotional development of the human being is with the work of Freud (1924, 1933, 1935). Freud posited different maturational phases to correspond with chronological development (see Table 2–3). He summarized these phases in pre-Oedipal, Oedipal, and Resolution phases and described the emotional attachments and behaviors resulting from the continuous battles between the libido and ego. As can be seen, the highest level of development occurs during the genital stage when the Oedipal Conflict is resolved. During this stage, the "fully functioning" male and female emphasize full primacy of the procreative sexual function with love as the object and the opposite sex as the love object. Another characteristic of the fully functioning person is the ability to love and to hate without ambivalence. In addition, the individual develops social feelings and is in full contact with reality.

Freud's hypotheses assert that since humans are governed by rudimentary instincts, they are destined to become victims of the interaction and conflict between these instincts and social forces. He further postulates that the only real hope for humans is to achieve and then diligently maintain a tolerable balance between internal impulses and external demands and restrictions.

Kratwohl and Bloom (1964) developed a scientific classification of the affective domain (see Table 2–4) that provides a sequencing of categories. The major characteristics of these categories are (1) an increasing emotional quality of responses, (2) responses becoming

TABLE 2-3   Freud's phases of psychosexual development

| Phase | Age | LIBIDO | | | |
		Libidinal stages		Narcissism	Antitheses
Pre-Oedipal	1	Oral	I	sucking	
	2		II	biting, devouring	
Oedipal	3	Anal- Sadistic	I	partial uncooperation	
				expulsion	active-passive
			II	partial love	
				retention	
	4–6	Phallic		primacy of phallic genital	phallic- castrated
	7–10	Latency		desexuality	
Resolution	11–12	Genital		full primacy of procreative sexual function	male- female

more automatic as one progresses up the continuum, (3) increasing willingness to attend to a specified stimulus, and (4) developing integration of a value pattern at the upper levels of the continuum. The overall organizing principle of the Kratwohl and Bloom classification in the process of development is referred to as *internalization.* The term refers to the inner growth that occurs as the individual becomes aware of and then adopts the attitudes, principles, codes, and sanctions that become a part of him or her in forming value judgments and in guiding his or her conduct (Kratwohl, 1964).

Another potentially important dimension of emotional development is seen in the work of Kohlberg (1960, 1963, 1964) on moral or ethical development. Kohlberg demonstrates the hierarchal nature of moral development (see Table 2–5). He ties it to a series of constructs of cognition that shift from simple to complex and indicates that thought progresses through the moral levels and is

AMBIVALENCE		EGO	
Object	*Topography*	*Inhibition formation*	*Reality*
auto-erotic	auto-erotic		magic
total uncooperation	narcissism	*anxiety*	omnipotence
partial love	ego	*fear (loss of love)*	magic
partial love	ego	*compassion-disgust*	reality-testing
object love	superego	*shame*	*reality principle*
inhibition		*guilt*	
object love		*social feelings*	reality principle

characterized by increasing integration. Kohlberg assumes that the two requisite factors for developing a moral understanding are (1) the opportunity for an open, interpersonal interaction between people who are not more than one level apart and (2) a situation structured to provide some value conflict between those people.

Harlow's work (1959, 1962) with primates also led him into the realm of interpersonal development. He distinguished between the development of "affection" and "sexual feelings," responses that Freud considered interdependent (see Table 2–6). His theory is based broadly on the positive responsiveness of adults toward infants, juveniles, and other members of these particular groups. At the highest level of functioning, the parental affectional system dominates. Broadly defined, the parental affectional system emphasizes positive responsiveness of adults toward infants, juveniles, and other members of their particular social groups.

TABLE 2-4 Synopsis of the taxonomy of educational objectives: affective domain (49)

1.0 Receiving (Attending). Sensitivity to the existence of certain phenomena and stimuli.
    1.1 Awareness. Learner is conscious of stimuli.
    1.2 Willingness to receive. Involves suspended judgment.
    1.3 Controlled or selected attention. Differentiation of stimulus.

2.0 Responding. Active attention to stimuli; e.g., compliance and commitment to rules and practices.
    2.1 Acquiescence in responding.
    2.2 Willingness to respond.
    2.3 Satisfaction in response.

3.0 Valuing. Consistent belief and attitude of worth held about a phenomenon.
    3.1 Acceptance of a value.
    3.2 Preference for a value.
    3.3 Commitment.

4.0 Organization. Organizing, interrelating, and analyzing different relevant values.
    4.1 Conceptualizing of a value.
    4.2 Organization of a value system.

5.0 Characterization by a value or value concept. Behavior is guided by values.
    5.1 Generalized set.
    5.2 Characterization.

Sullivan (1953) extended Freud's psycholosexual phases into the interpersonal realm (see Table 2-7). His work defines interpersonal development as essentially culture free and describes interpersonal motivation as a hierarchy of increasing complexity in the sophistication of interactions between dependence and independence. Interpersonal motivation also increases the potential for interdependence. Sullivan asserts that it is the satisfactory articulation of independent self-validation and dependent social validation that makes it possible for the individual to be true to self on the one hand and receptive to others on the other hand. It is from this interplay between appropriate interactive dependence and independence that interdependence emerges. The predominantly interdependent person has both the ability to be dependent and independent as each is appropriate. Interdependent people are able to use their own resources and also to bid successfully for the resources of others to reach mutually rewarding goals.

TABLE 2-5 Kohlberg's stages of moral development

Level I	PRECONVENTIONAL (pre-moral)	Stage 1.	Obey rules to avoid punishment: The value of a human life is confused with the value of physical objects and is based on the social status or physical attributes of its possessor.
		Stage 2.	Conform to obtain rewards, have favors returned: The value of a human life is seen as instrumental to the satisfaction of the needs of its possessor or of other persons.
Level II	CONVENTIONAL (role conformity)	Stage 3.	Conform to avoid disapproval, dislike by others: The value of a human life is based on the empathy and affection of family members and others toward its possessor.
		Stage 4.	Conform to avoid censure by legitimate authorities and resultant guilt: Life is conceived as sacred in terms of its place in a categorical moral or religious order of rights and duties.
Level III	POSTCONVENTIONAL (self-accepted moral principles)	Stage 5.	Conform to maintain the respect of the impartial spectator judging in terms of community welfare: Life is valued both in terms of its relation to community welfare and in terms of life being a universal human right.
		Stage 6.	Conform to avoid self-condemnation: Belief in the sacredness of human life as representing a universal human value of respect for the individual.

TABLE 2-6 Harlow's five affectional systems

1. The *infant-mother* affectional system, which binds the infant to the mother.

2. The *mother-infant* affectional system, or maternal affectional system.

3. The *infant-infant, age-mate,* or peer affectional system, through which infants and children interrelate and develop persisting affection for each other.

4. The *sexual and heterosexual* affectional system, culminating in adolescent sexuality and finally in those adult behaviors leading to procreation.

5. The *paternal* affectional system, broadly defined in terms of positive responsiveness of adult males toward infants, juveniles, and other members of their particular social groups.

With Flanders's (1965) scientific classification of interaction, the interrelationship of emotion and intellect begins to appear (see Table 2–8). Although this interaction analysis is sufficiently general to create difficulties in interpretation, with modification, it has proven to be quite useful as a classroom observation scale. As can be

TABLE 2-7 Sullivan's phases in interpersonal development

Age	Characteristics
Birth	Prototaxic: Infant "is" the world.
Infancy	Parataxic: Articulate speech (however uncommunicative) as an interpersonal motivator.
Childhood	Appearance of need for playmates; i.e., companions, cooperative peer beings.
Juvenile era	Syntaxic: Interpersonal social validation. From need for peers to need for an intimate relationship with one other of comparable status.
Preadolescence	From strong interest in relationship with peer of same sex to strong interest in relationship with peer of opposite sex.
Adolescence	Some type of satisfying sexual performance.
Late adolescence	Partially developed aspects of personality become organized in appropriate time and space.
Adulthood	Love relationship with significant other, as significant, or nearly as significant as oneself.

seen, the analysis categorizes the indirect and direct influences of a teacher or helper as well as responsive and initiative student talk. There has been evidence to suggest that, with learners under specifiable teaching conditions, the indirect approach of accepting feelings, praising, and encouraging is most facilitative in affecting learner development.

TABLE 2-8   Flanders's interaction analysis

Teacher Talk	Indirect Influence	1. *Accepts feelings:* Accepts and clarifies the feeling tone of the students in a nonthreatening manner. Feelings may be positive or negative. Predicting or recalling feelings are included.
		2. *Praises or encourages:* Praises or encourages student action or behavior. Jokes that release tension, not at the expense of another individual, nodding head or saying, "um hum" or "go on" are included.
		3. *Accepts or uses ideas of students:* Clarifying, building, or developing ideas suggested by a student. As teacher brings more of his or her own ideas into play, shift to Category 5.
		4. *Asks questions:* Asking a question about content or procedure with the intent that a student answer.
	Direct Influence	5. *Lecturing:* Giving facts or opinions about content or procedure; expressing own ideas, asking rhetorical questions.
		6. *Giving directions:* Directions, commands, or orders to which a student is expected to comply.
		7. *Criticizing or justifying authority:* Statements intended to change student behavior from nonacceptable to acceptable pattern; severe criticism of student's behavior; statements why the teacher is doing what he or she is doing; extreme self-reference.
Student Talk		8. *Student talk—response:* Talk by students in response to teacher. Teacher initiates the contact or solicits student statement.
		9. *Student talk—initiation:* Talk by students that they initiate. If "calling on" student is only to indicate who may talk next, observer must decide whether student wanted to talk. If he or she did, use this category.
		10. *Silence or confusion:* Pauses, short periods of silence, and periods of confusion in which communication cannot be understood by the observer.

The potential for enhancing motivation through the conscious development of affective skills is great. Interpersonal communication skills are now describable and teachable and evidence has been built up in support of their effect upon both the emotional and the intellectual realms of functioning (Carkhuff, 1969; Carkhuff and Berenson, 1976). Together, the emotional-interpersonal skill areas of human functioning constitute important dimensions of actualizing human potential.

INTELLECTUAL DEVELOPMENT

Intellectual development is perhaps the most represented and least understood area of human development. There is as yet no commonly accepted developmental sequence of cognition, but by looking at some prevalent theories, specific characteristics emerge. Among the characteristics of cognitive development are processing ideas; analyzing, evaluating, synthesizing, and predicting; creating ideas, relationships, applications, and products; testing reality; and making real-life applications (including the use of both data and cognitive strategies in solving life problems).

Piaget (1950, 1952, 1969) posited in his thesis that there are indeed developmental stages associated with certain age ranges

TABLE 2-9   Piaget's scale of cognitive development

Age	Stage	Operations
birth–2	Sensori-motor stage	Mute—no use of verbal symbols Learns to perceive—discriminate and identify objects.
2–7	Preoperational stage	Symbols and representations— Acts on perceptive impulses— Static-irreversible thinking.
7–11	Concrete operations stage	Analyzing—Conscious of dynamic variables—Classifies things in groups or series.
11–on	Formal operations stage	Abstract-conceptual thinking— Reasoning generalized; evaluation; hypothesizing; imagining; synthesizing.

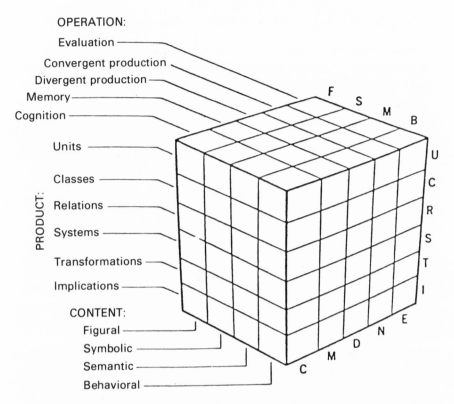

FIGURE 2-1   Guilford's structure of the intellectual model

(see Table 2-9). As can be seen, Piaget's hierarchy emphasizes sensorimotor development in infancy; pre-operational or symbolic learning in early childhood; concrete operations in later childhood; and formal operations from age eleven on. The highest level of cognitive development involves abstract-conceptual thinking, generalized reasoning, evaluation, hypothesizing, imagining, and synthesizing—all the tools requisite for fully functioning adult behavior.

Guilford's structure of intellect model is most inclusive and provides an empirical point of reference (1956, 1967). The model, a psychometric one derived from intercorrelations between performance data on a variety of abilities, is based upon factors along three dimensions (see Figure 2-1). The intersection of these factors defines many different potential abilities. The model has produced evidence supporting the relationship of divergent thinking ability and academic success. In addition, it amassed support for the separate dimensionalities of creativity and intelligence. Some educators feel that this model provides a more accurate demonstration of the creative process than do intelligence and achievement measures. Perhaps most important, Guilford's work has been a model of operationalization for investigators who have simulated the human brain in the development of information-processing models.

Dewey's views of logical thinking provide a valuable model for problem-solving (1910). His five-step model continues to be of heuristic value (see Table 2–10). As such, it represents one of the oldest conceptions of the nature of thought concerned with the logical stages or distinct steps involved in a complex thinking act. The steps are cumulative and range from recognizing and analyzing the problem through generating solutions and testing consequences to judging selected solutions.

Classifications of cognitive processes have another kind of empirical base and these are based on task analysis. Gagne's learning model stems from task analysis research and concerns different qualitative performances that serve as prerequisites for complex tasks (1959, 1965). Gagne's model is a classification of a variety of learning paradigms (see Table 2–11). According to Gagne, learning a simple stimulus response chain is easier than learning to solve a problem. In each case, conditions under which the learning occurs, the nature of the response, and the internal conditions of the learner are necessarily different. At the highest levels of Gagne's cumulative learning model, the learning type emphasizes higher order problem-solving including self-arousal and selection of previously learned rules to achieve novel combinations. (In contrast to Guilford's problem-solving models and information-processing models, Gagne's cumulative learning model deals with thought processes as

TABLE 2-10   Dewey's five-step problem-solving model

1. A felt difficulty (*recognize problem*)

2. Location and definition (*analyze problem*)

3. Suggestion of a possible solution (*generate solution*)

4. Development by reasoning of the bearings of the suggestion (*test consequences*)

5. Further observation and experiment leading to its acceptance or rejection (*judge selected solutions*)

TABLE 2-11 Gagné's summary of essential conditions appropriate for each type of learning

Learning type	Prerequisite capability	External conditions of learning
Ss→R connection	Apprehension of stimulus	Presentation of stimulus so that desired response will be contiguous in time and supply contingent reinforcement.
Motor chain	Individual connections	A sequence of external cues, stimulating a sequence of specific responses contiguous in time; repetition for selection of correct response-produced stimuli.
Verbal chain	Individual connections including "coding" links	A sequence of external verbal cues, stimulating a sequence of verbal responses contiguous in time; repetition may be necessary to reduce interference.
Discrimination	Apprehension of stimulus	Practice providing contrast of correct and incorrect stimuli; or, practice providing progressive reduction in stimulus differences.
Concrete concept	Discriminations	Responding to a variety of stimuli differing in appearance, belonging to a single class.
Rule, including defined concepts	Concepts	External cues, usually verbal, stimulate the formation of component concepts contiguously in a proper sequence; application is made in specific examples.
Higher-order rule —Problem solving	Rules	Self-arousal and selection of previously learned rules to achieve a novel combination.

they are characterized by performance, expression, and particular conditions prerequisite for the emergence of the processes.)

Another model based upon task analysis is Bloom's scientific classification of educational objectives in the cognitive domain (1956). Rather than being a classification of a variety of learning paradigms, it is the classification of a wide variety of educational objectives (see Table 2-12). It is primarily concerned with analyzing learning task content as it applies to the more abstract goals of instruction. Bloom's model is a descriptive one. Whatever hierarchical qualities are attributed to it are logical not psychological. Again, in contrast to Guilford's model, Bloom's classification is sufficiently general to create difficulties in interpretation. Still, it has proven to be of immense value as a classroom observation scale. It is best used by curriculum planners as a reference rather than as a framework for the derivation of objectives.

In summary, cognitive concerns and theories are evident within various subject matter disciplines. These disciplines generate additional approaches to cognitive development such as trans-

TABLE 2-12 Synopsis of the taxonomy of educational objectives: cognitive domain (7)

KNOWLEDGE

1.00 *Knowledge.* Recall of information.
1.10 Knowledge of specifics. Emphasis is on symbols with concrete referents.
　　1.11 Knowledge of terminology.
　　1.12 Knowledge of specific facts.
1.20 Knowledge of ways and means of dealing with specifics. Includes methods of inquiry, chronological sequences, standards of judgment, patterns of organization within a field.
　　1.21 Knowledge of conventions: Accepted usage, correct style, etc.
　　1.22 Knowledge of trends and sequences.
　　1.23 Knowledge of classifications and categories.
　　1.24 Knowledge of criteria.
　　1.25 Knowledge of methodology for investigating particular problems.

KNOWLEDGE

1.30 Knowledge of the universals and abstractions in a field. Patterns and schemes by which phenomena and ideas are organized.
　　1.31 Knowledge of principles and generalizations.
　　1.32 Knowledge of theories and structures (as a connected body of principles, generalizations, and interrelations).

INTELLECTUAL SKILLS AND ABILITIES

2.00 *Comprehension.* Understanding of material being communicated, without necessarily relating it to other material.

2.10 Translation. From one set of symbols to another.

2.20 Interpretation. Summarization or explanation of a communication.

2.30 Extrapolation. Extension of trends beyond the given data.

3.00 *Application.* The use of abstractions in particular, concrete situations.

4.00 *Analysis.* Breaking a communication into its parts so that organization of ideas is clear.

4.10 Analysis of elements; e.g., recognizing assumptions.

4.20 Analysis of relationships. Content or mechanical factors.

4.30 Analysis of organizational principles. What holds the communication together?

5.00 *Synthesis.* Putting elements into a whole.

5.10 Production of a unique communication.

5.20 Production of a plan for operations.

5.30 Derivation of a set of abstract relations.

6.00 *Evaluation.* Judging the value of material for a given purpose.

6.10 Judgments in terms of internal evidence; e.g., logical consistency.

6.20 Judgments in terms of external evidence; e.g., consistency with facts developed elsewhere.

formational grammar and general semantics. Although there is a lack of agreement about cognitive human development, these studies provide important implications for cognitive curriculum.

SUMMARY AND OVERVIEW

Perhaps the greatest value of all of these developmental models is their heuristic value. They enable us to deduce and test our hypothesis and to use the feedback to refine the original formulations. When we begin to integrate these models for our understanding and operationalization of the processes and outcomes of actualizing human potential, we find their dimensions of great value. Certainly, the "physiological actualization" programs that enable us to begin to describe, predict, and control our own bodily functions as a means of developing a whole person are promising. Fitness programs promising an increasing yield in the physical energy necessary for physical, emotional, and intellectual functioning are critical.

In the area of emotional development, the work of Freud continues to be one of the most stimulating theories in terms of theoretical and rehabilitation developments. The models of Bloom and Kohlberg have been most valuable for understanding the development of values that organize and motivate people to behave in the interpersonal realm. Harlow and Sullivan have helped us to understand the levels of interpersonal development and Flanders has begun to help us understand the interactions that go on between people.

In the area of intellectual development, Piaget, like Freud in the emotional realm, has provided significant sources of stimulation for model-building and child-rearing practices. Dewey and Gagne give us the learning principles of problem-solving and program development; Guilford gives us a model for operationalizing cognitive goals while others move toward the development of a technology for both operationalizing goals and technologizing the means to achieve those goals; and Bloom, like Flanders in the affective domain, gives us a useful taxonomy for cognitive functioning.

In the largest perspective of motivation, the greatest distinguishing characteristics are those involving the skills and knowledge development of the adult. The movement toward the actualization of adulthood or human potential involves the development of specific sets of skills and knowledge—physical fitness skills that increase the energy reservoirs, emotional and interpersonal skills that expand the boundaries of one's humanity, intellectual skills that enable us to develop and implement the operations to achieve goals in our worlds. Together, these physical, emotional, and intellectual skills define the fully functioning human being. These dimensions constitute the ingredients of any formula for actualizing human potential.

REFERENCES

Agazarian, Y. M.; Boyer, E. G.; Simon, A.; and White, P. *Documenting Development*. Philadelphia: Research for Better Schools, 1972.

Bloom, B. S.; Englehart, M.D.; Furst, E. J.; Hill, W. H.; and Krathwohl, D. R. *A Taxonomy of Educational Objectives. Handbook I: The Cognitive Domain*. New York: Longmans, Green, 1956.

Carkhuff, R. R. *Helping and Human Relations. Vols. I and II*. New York: Holt, Rinehart and Winston, 1969.

Carkhuff, R. R. and Berenson, B. G. *Teaching as Treatment*. Amherst, Mass.: Human Resource Development Press, 1976.

Collingwood, T. R. "Human Resource Development and Physical Fitness." In D. Kratochvil (Ed.) *Carkhuff: The HRD Model in Education.* Baton Rouge: Southern University Press, 1973.

Dewey, J. *How We Think.* Boston: D.C. Heath, 1910.

Flanders, N. A. *Interaction Analyses in the Classroom.* Ann Arbor: University of Michigan Press, 1965.

Freud, S. *Collected Papers.* London: Hogarth, 1924.

———— . *New Introductory Lectures.* New York: Norton, 1933.

———— . *The Ego and the Id.* London and New York: Hogarth, 1935.

Gagne, R. M. "Problem Solving and Thinking." *Annual Review of Psychology,* 1954, *10,* 147–172.

———— . *The Conditions of Learning.* New York: Holt, Rinehart and Winston, 1965.

Guilford, J. P. "The Structure of Intellect." *Psychological Bulletin,* 1956, *53,* 267–293.

———— . *The Nature of Human Intelligence.* New York: McGraw-Hill, 1967.

Harlow, A. F. and Zimmerman, R. R. "Affectional Responses in the Infant Monkey." *Science,* 1959, *130,* 421–432.

Harlow, H. F. and Harlow, M. K. "Social Deprivation in Monkeys." *Scientific American,* 1962, *207,* 137–146.

Kohlberg, L. A. "The Development of Children's Orientations Toward a Moral Order," *Vita Humano,* 1960, *6,* 11–33.

———— . "Early Education: A Cognitive-Developmental View." *Child Development,* 1968, *39,* 1013–1062.

———— . "Development of Moral Character and Moral Idealogy." *Review of Child Development Research, Vol. I.* M. L. Hoffman and L. W. Hoffman (Eds.). New York: Russell Sage Foundation, 1964.

Kratwohl, D. R.; Bloom, B. S.; Englehart, M. D.; Furst, E. J.; and Hull, W. H. *Taxonomy of Educational Objectives. Handbook II: The Affective Domain.* New York: David McKay and Company, 1964.

Piaget, J. *The Psychology of Intelligence.* London: Routledge and Kegan, Paul, 1950.

———— . *The Origins of Intelligence in Children.* New York: International Universities Press, 1952.

Piaget, J. and Inhelder, B. *The Psychology of the Child.* New York: Basic Books, 1969.

Sullivan, H. S. *The Interpersonal Theory of Psychiatry.* New York: Norton, 1953.

3
Some principles
of actualizing

When we created our "do tank," a "think tank" geared toward developing the human technologies and systems needed to deliver tangible human benefits, we sought out a facilitative environment. We found an old mill, overlooking a mill pond and a waterfall. We knocked down all of the walls and created a free and open physical environment. Psychologically and intellectually, we followed this model. We created a climate of trust and openness, providing free access to all information and conducting inservice seminars to freely share all skills. Some of the people working there began to attempt to actualize themselves. Their immediate effectiveness depended upon their initial levels of functioning. Those operating at the incentive level satisfied their needs for belonging and self-acceptance. Those operating with achievement motivation realized their self- and product-worth. Those operating with a need to actualize themselves became interdependent and creative producers of products and achievers of objectives. Some few, beginning at whatever levels, made their way through the succeeding levels to achieve their mission in life.

Maslow (1964, 1968, 1970, 1972), more than any other human of his time, probed the dimensions of human potential. What he came up with were some principles describing the subjective experience and objective reality of people whom he viewed as self-actualized people. In so doing, he went far beyond his data. Most important, he did not give us an operational means to achieve these dimensions.

Maslow's self-actualized people were well recognized public and historical figures, including Eleanor Roosevelt, Jane Adams, William James, Albert Schweitzer, Aldous Huxley, and Spinoza. Other historical figures included Abraham Lincoln and Thomas Jefferson and a long list of potential or possible cases suggested or studied by others. While the choice of these figures—all of whom espoused a liberal values system—became somewhat controversial, Maslow's work set the standard for studying the process and products of self-actualization. Maslow's studies of self-actualizers grew out of his earlier work on understanding the basic needs of humans.

THE NEED HIERARCHY

Maslow's work on motivation culminated in the development of a *need hierarchy*. Drawing from the functional roots in James and Dewey; the holistic roots in Wertheimer, Goldstein, and Gestalt psychology; and the psychodynamic roots in Freud, Fromm, Horney, Reich, Jung, and Adler, Maslow postulated several basic human needs (See Figure 3-1).

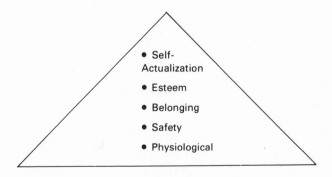

Figure 3-1   Maslow's need hierarchy

Physiological needs

As can be seen, physiological needs constitute the base of the need hierarchy. These needs are considered prepotent; that is, lacking everything else, basic physiological needs for food and water will dominate. Further, if all other needs are unsatisfied and the organism is thus dominated by physiological needs, all other needs do not exist for the organism. We can, then, characterize the whole organism as hungry, for consciousness is almost completely preempted by hunger. All human capacities are put into the service of hunger-satisfaction, and the organization of these capacities is almost entirely determined by its own purpose of satisfying hunger.

Safety needs

When the basic physiological needs are met, other higher needs emerge. Primary among those emerging are safety needs—including the need for security; stability; dependency; protection; freedom from fear, anxiety, and chaos; and structure, order, law, and limits. Just as with physiological needs, the organism may be dominated by safety needs, so that they become almost exclusive organizers of behavior, recruiting all of the capacities of the organism in their service. Maslow concluded that the average person, adult as well as child, prefers a safe, orderly, predictable, lawful, organized world, which he or she can count on. In such a world, unexpected, unmanageable, chaotic or other dangerous things do not happen and powerful protectors will shield him or her from harm.

Belongingness and love needs

If both physiological and safety needs are met, a need for love and affection and belongingness emerges. This need becomes the new center of self-organization and the person hungers for affectionate relations with people in general and for a place in his or her group or family in specific. At this level, he or she will also feel sharply the pangs of loneliness, ostracism, and rejection. In this context, Maslow hypothesized that personal growth groups, intentional communities, and even, to some degree, youth rebellion groups have grown out of a need to satisfy belongingness. He also distinguished love from sex needs and emphasized that the love need involved both giving and receiving love.

Esteem needs

The other needs being satisfied, esteem needs emerge. Here Maslow classified esteem needs into two subsidiary sets. The first emphasized self-esteem and involved the desire for strength, achievement, adequacy, and mastery. He also included the need for independence and freedom in this category. The second category emphasized esteem from others and included the desire for reputation or prestige, status, fame, glory, dominance, recognition, attention, importance, dignity, and appreciation. Satisfaction of the esteem needs leads to feelings of competence and confidence in facing the world, while the thwarting of these needs produces feelings of inferiority and helplessness.

Self-actualization

Finally, the needs for self-actualization may emerge for those few who have satisfied all prior needs. Maslow defined self-actualization in terms of the person's "desire for self-fulfillment, namely, to the tendency for him to become actualized in what he is potentially." He elaborated on this definition as "the desire to become more and more what one idiosyncratically is, to become everything that one is capable of becoming." Maslow acknowledged that the specific form these needs take will vary greatly from person to person. "In one individual it may take the form of the desire to be an ideal mother, in another it may be expressed athletically and in still another it may be expressed in painting pictures or in inventions. At this level, individual differences are greatest."

MOTIVATION

The relationship of the need hierarchy to motivation can be seen in Table 3-1. As can be seen, environmental influences affect all phases of development. In self-actualizing development, the environment has as much to do with the mastery of different phases of development as do the internal integrations of the environment. It is clear that each level of need can be aroused through deprivation of satisfaction at that level. Whenever a need becomes reactivated, resolution is again required if mastery of the earlier level is to be gained so that more sophisticated functioning can be measured.

TABLE 3-1 Maslow's hierarchy of needs in relation to motivation

Internal needs	Motivation	Response to satisfied need	Response to unsatisfied need
Self-Actualization (creativity)	Expert resources (sharing skills and knowledge) ▲ Working for planned change or gain.	Interdependent Creative/effective	Project anxiety Defense: Revert to independence
Esteem (achievement)	Reward (praise) ▲ Work for approval.	Self-worth Product value	Social anxiety Defense: Reactive conformity or nonconformity
Belonging (affiliation)	Reward (affection) ▲ Work for love.	Acceptance of self Acceptance of others	Separation anxiety Defense: overpersonal or counterpersonal
Safety (security)	Punishment (threat) ▲ Work to avoid punishment.	Self-control Self-confidence	Fear of helplessness Defense: Dependence or counterdependence
Physiological (survival)	Punishment (physical) ▲ Work to avoid repetition of punishment.	Sense of self Differentiation from environment	Annihilation anxiety Defense: Outward conformity

Mastery of the physiological or survival level is characterized by a sense of identity, of self, of the inner person—a sense of location in terms of one's own body boundaries and one's own autonomy and potentiality. Feelings of self or basic trust, autonomy, and control of impulses are developed in the person when feelings of trust, autonomy, and self-control are communicated from the environment. Whenever physical punishment is used, survival is threatened and obedience in the form of outward passive conformity and inward immobilization emerges. The inner experiences of immobilization, undifferentiated panic states and annihilation anxiety, feelings of being overwhelmed, impairment of the ability to discriminate between oneself and others, fear of being dependent or independent, fear of loss of identity, and fear of fusion are all symptoms of regression to the survival level. To regain mastery of the physiological survival level, a person must regain a sense of self as a separate identity in the surrounding environment.

Mastery and resolution of the safety or security phase is dependent upon the ability to perceive similarities in the apparently dissimilar and dissimilarities in the apparently similar. This increased quality of perception permits greater complexity of both affective and cognitive responses. The ability to process phenomena of greater complexity opens the way to the confidence that comes with handling new experiences efficiently. Mastery of safety is characterized by a sense of control, both a feeling of self-control and also a feeling of being in control. Confidence comes from the development of tolerance to frustration, which enhances the ability to delay acting on impulse and elicits the collection of data instead. However, to the extent that providing safety and security becomes a goal in itself, rather than one of the factors that expand the kinds of goals that can be set, life is organized in terms of defense against fears of insecurity. Activating the need for safety impairs the process of mastery, and fears of helplessness and being out of control emerge. Defensive reactions, such as dependent, compulsive obedience and its reciprocal, compulsive counterdependent rebellion, are aroused.

Mastery of the belonging or affiliative phase of development is dependent upon the ability to distinguish between oneself and others and to perceive individual differences and to relate appropriately to different roles. Mastery of belonging is found in interpersonal love, affection, and sex. The person who is secure at the belonging level is the person who can respond appropriately in relation to others. Successful interpersonal relationships build feelings of adequacy, self-esteem, and the feeling of being a full person. The need for belonging is fulfilled when there is an accepting climate that receives people as autonomous and special. However, using love or esteem as a way of controlling people is likely to activate the need for affiliation. When love becomes contingent upon certain levels of performance, fear of loss of love is aroused and counterpersonal or overpersonal defensiveness is activated in response to an unsatisfied belonging need.

Mastery at the esteem or ego level frees a person to act because he or she chooses to do so, not because he or she needs to do so. This intentional action creates a satisfaction in doing, which is part of actualizing self. Mastery of esteem level needs is dependent upon the ability to differentiate between who one is and what one does. Central to this mastery is the ability to objectify and evaluate personal production without feeling that one's self gains or loses value based on the findings. The motivation to achieve through setting goals and solving problems characterizes these ego level functions. Ego anxieties are mobilized when praise of person and not product is used as the major motivation for production. Sometimes when ego anxieties are aroused, nonconforming, antisocial behaviors appear along with the denial of any wish for approval or any need for acceptance. Instead, inappropriate demands are made upon others to conform to the person's expectations or values. Oversocialized and antisocial behaviors are inverse reactions to the same stress.

People functioning at the level of self-actualization tend to be very creative and productive people. They are interdependent in their reception and contribution to input and feedback for all of their actions. They are experiential, experimental, and operational in their orientation to all new learnings. Mastery at this level is dependent upon cooperative harmony between the various levels of need within the individual and between people. Self-actualization is a function of synergistic inner-personal and interpersonal relationships. When relationships, both within and between people are characterized by synergistic interdependence, people interact with others and the situation—not only in the service of themselves but also in the service of others as well as the situational objectives. Self-actualization is encouraged in a climate of trust and openness, where appropriate information and skills are shared, and personally and socially validatable responses that make possible a system of negative entropy are generated. In closed, suspicious, or strategizing climates, self-actualization creativity is inhibited and inhibition is manifested by frustration at external or internal limits. Regression from the level of interdependent self-actualization is not to the esteem or belonging needs level but to the independent self-actualization level. That is to say, the independent actualizer is functioning at levels lower than the interdependent actualizer.

SELF-ACTUALIZING PEOPLE

Maslow expanded to study the nature of self-actualized people—in part for its heuristic value but perhaps primarily for actualization purposes of his own. His subjects were selected from among personal acquaintances and public and historical figures. After researching college students, he concluded that self-actualization of the sort found in older subjects was not possible in our society for young, developing people. Using criteria including the absence of neuroses as determined by projective testing, Maslow defined self-actualization as "the full use and exploration of talents, capacities, potentialities, etc." This criterion implied the gratification of the basic physiological, safety, belonging, and esteem needs. Data was gathered in the form of global or holistic impressions based upon iterations of refining the dimensions of self-actualization. Composite impressions were offered for fifteen important and useful whole characteristics of self-actualizing people.

Accurate reality perceptions

This capacity involves the ability of self-actualized persons to discriminate effectively. Beginning initially as a capacity to discern other people accurately, this dimension evolves as an ability to see concealed or confused realities more swiftly and correctly than others do. Their predictions of the future from whatever facts are at hand seem to be more often correct—because these predictions are not confused with wish, desire, anxiety, fear, or a generalized optimism or pessimism. Maslow drew support for this dimension from the absolute inefficiency of the neurotic person: "The neurotic is not emotionally sick—he is cognitively wrong!" In this context, self-actualizing people distinguish far more easily than most the fresh, concrete, and idiographic from the generic, abstract, and rubricized. The consequence is that they live more in the real world of nature than in the man-made mass of concepts, abstractions, expectations, beliefs, and stereotypes that most people confuse with the world.

Acceptance

Healthy individuals accept themselves and their own nature without chagrin or complaint. They are free of the crippling guilt, shame, or anxiety of the dysfunctional people around them. They accept themselves and others in stoic style, complete with all their shortcomings and discrepancies from an ideal image. "What we must say rather is that they can take the frailties and sins, weaknesses and evils of human nature in the same unquestioning spirit with which one accepts the characteristics of nature." Closely related to self- and other-acceptance is their lack of defensiveness, protective color- ation, or pose. About the only things that healthy people feel guilty about are improvable shortcomings in conditioned habits: "The general formula seems to be that healthy people will feel bad about discrepancies between what is and what might very well be or ought to be."

Spontaneity

Self-actualizing people are spontaneous in external behavior and internal thoughts and impulses. Their behavior is characterized by simplicity and naturalness and by lack of artificiality or straining for effect. However, they are not typically as unconventional in their behavior as in their thoughts: "Apparently recognizing that the world of people in which he lives could not understand or accept this, and since he has no wish to hurt them or to fight with them over every triviality, he will go through the ceremonies and rituals of con- vention with a good-humored shrug and with the best possible grace." In this context, Maslow found that the motivational life of self-actualizing people is not only quantitatively different but also qualitatively different from that of ordinary people. The motivation of non-self-actualizing people is to gratify basic needs. The motiva- tion of actualizing people is to attempt to grow to perfection and to develop more and more fully in their own style—in a word, self- actualization.

Problem centering

In general, actualizing people focus upon problems or tasks outside of themselves; that is, they are problem-centered rather than ego- centered. They, themselves, are not problems for themselves. They have some missions in life, some purpose to fulfill, some problem outside of themselves that enlists their energies. Their tasks are not necessarily tasks that they would prefer or choose for themselves but often are tasks that they feel are their responsibility. In general, these tasks are nonpersonal or unselfish, concerned rather with the good of humankind in general or of groups or individuals specifically.

Detachment and privacy

Actualizing people also appear to have an ability to be solitary without harm to themselves and without discomfort. Indeed, they enjoy solitude and privacy to a definitely greater degree than the average person. It is often possible for them to remain above the battle, to remain unruffled, undisturbed by the turmoil around them. They are at once aloof and reserved, calm and serene. They do not personalize their misfortunes and never react violently as most people do. They retain their dignity even in undignified situations, at least in part because of their tendency to interpret those situations. Maslow suggests that self-actualizing people do not need others in the ordinary sense and that this detachment is not easily accepted by most people. He concludes that such individuals have more "free will" and are less "determined" than others.

Autonomy

Self-actualizing people are also relatively independent of their physical and social environments: "Since they are propelled by growth motivation rather than by deficiency motivation, self-actualizing people are not dependent for their main satisfactions on the real world, or other people or culture or means to ends or, in general, on extrinsic satisfactions." Rather, they are dependent upon their own resources and potentials. Again, this independence means a relative stability in the face of hard times and frustrations. These people maintain a relative serenity in the midst of circumstances that would immobilize other people.

Freshness of appreciation

"Self-actualizing people have the wonderful capacity to appreciate again and again, freshly and naively, the basic goods of life, with awe, pleasure, wonder, and even ecstacy, however stale these experiences may have become to others..." For such people, even the workaday world and the moment-to-moment business of living can be thrilling and exciting. They are people who really do count their blessings in an immediacy and intensity of experiencing. Maslow supports his conclusions with citations of a number of studies indicating an improvement in the quality of life with an improvement in the recognition of its quality.

Mystic experiencing

Not unrelated are the experiences Maslow calls *mystic experiencing*. Sometimes the emotions become strong enough to be called mystic experiences. Maslow described these experiences as "limitless horizons opening up to the vision, the feeling of being simultaneously more powerful and also more helpless than one ever was before, the feeling of great ecstacy and wonder and awe, the loss of placing of time and space with, finally, the conviction that something extremely important and valuable had happened, so that the subject is to some extent transformed and strengthened even in his daily life by such experience." The acute mystic or peak experience is an intensification of any experiences in which there is a loss of self or a transcendence of it. Maslow predicted that healthy, non-peaking self-actualizers would be social world improvers while transcending peakers would be found in the arts and religion.

Identification with humanity (gemenischaftsgefühl)

Self-actualizers have for human beings, in general, a deep feeling of identification and affection. Because of this, according to Maslow, they have a genuine desire to help the human race. They see everyone as members of a single family although as members of the family, they occasionally get impatient and even disgusted with them:

> When it comes down to it, in certain ways he is like an alien in a strange land. Very few really understand him, however much they may like him. He is often saddened, exasperated, and even enraged, by the shortcomings of the average person, and while they are to him ordinarily no more than a nuisance, they sometimes become bitter tragedy. However far apart he is from them at times, he nevertheless feels a basic underlying kinship with these creatures whom he must regard with, if not condescension, at least the knowledge that he can do many things better than they can, that he can see things that they cannot see, that the truth that is so clear to him is for most people veiled and hidden (Maslow, 1970, p. 166).

Interpersonal relations

It is clear that self-actualizing people have deeper and more meaningful interpersonal relations than other adults: "They are capable of more fusion, greater love, more perfect identification, more obliteration of the ego boundaries than other people would consider possible." There are, however, some important qualifiers: Other parties to the relationships are healthier and closer to self-actualization. In general, these self-actualizers tend to be kind to everyone. They have a very tender love for children and a general compassion for all peoples. While they tend to attract admirers, the admirers are apt to demand more than the self-actualizers are willing to give. Any hostility that the self-actualizers evidence is not character-based or pathological, but is reactive or situational.

Democratic character structure

All self-actualizers are democratic people in the deepest sense of the word. They are friendly with anyone of suitable character. They learn from anyone who has anything to teach them—no matter what other characteristics he or she has. In this context, they are all quite well aware of how little they know in comparison with what could be known and what is known by other people. Here Maslow makes a careful distinction between democratic feeling and a lack of discrimination in taste: "These individuals, themselves elite, select for their friends elite, but this is an elite of character, capacity and talent, rather than of birth, race, blood, name, family, age, youth, fame or power."

Discriminating means and ends

Self-actualizers have a strong sense of right and wrong, of good and evil. They are more likely rather than less likely to counterattack against evil people and evil behavior. They are far less ambivalent about their own anger than others. They are strongly ethical, having definite moral standards. Needless to say, their notions of right and wrong are often not the conventional ones. For self-actualized people, the means and ends are clearly distinguishable. In general, they are focused upon ends and the means are subordinated to their purposes.

Sense of humor

The sense of humor of self-actualizers is not of the ordinary type. Characteristically, what they consider humor is more closely allied to philosophy than to anything else: "Such humor can be very pervasive; the human situation, human pride, seriousness, busy-ness, bustle, ambition, striving and planning can all be seen as amusing, even funny."

Creativeness

The universal characteristic of self-actualizers is creativity. Indeed, creativity is the way in which we judge who are self-actualizers and who are not. Each self-actualizer shows his or her creativity in unique ways. The creativeness seems to take the form of the creative products of unspoiled children: "Most human beings lose this as they become enculturated, but some few individuals seem either to retain this fresh and naive, direct way of looking at life, or if they have lost it, as most people do, they later in life recover it."

Resistance to enculturation

Self-actualizing people resist enculturation and maintain a certain inner detachment from the culture in which they are immersed. The relationship of these people with a less healthy culture has several components: (1) all self-actualizers fall well within the limits of apparent conventionality in appearance and behavior in our culture; (2) no self-actualizers are in rebellion against authority; (3) all self-actualizers are ruled by the laws of their character rather than by the rules of society. In sum, they manage to get along by a combination of inner autonomy and outer acceptance, a course that will be possible only so long as the culture remains tolerant of this kind of detached withholding from complete cultural identification.

SUMMARY AND CONCLUSIONS

In summary, Maslow elaborates the dimensions of self-actualizing people that he interviewed and studied. Since there are constant threads interwoven through many of them, it appears that there are a number of ways to organize the dimensions that he developed. The dimensions may be factored as:

Cultural dimensions
  Autonomy
  Resistance to enculturation
  Identification with humanity

Philosophical dimensions
   Accurate reality perceptions
   Detachment
   Sense of humor
Emotional dimensions
   Spontaneity
   Freshness of appreciation
   Mystic experiencing
Interpersonal dimensions
   Acceptance
   Interpersonal relations
   Democratic character structure
Intellectual dimensions
   Problem-centered
   Discriminating means and ends
   Creativity

Thus, we find self-actualizing dimensions evolving in clusters around critical factors—cultural or the independence of culture and the identification with humanity, philosophical or the constancy and accuracy of perceptions, emotional or the openness and immediacy of experiencing, interpersonal or the facilitative relations with others, and intellectual or the acuity of cognitive applications. The cultural and the philosophical dimensions speak to the attitudinal stance the self-actualizing person takes toward life. The attitudinal stance is independent of the everyday real world, yet it appears to see that real world in sharp perspective. The emotional and interpersonal factors, in turn, relate to the self-actualizing person's experience of self and others. The human system is always open—always facilitative. The final factor, the intellectual, is just that—the application of a sharp and creative intellect to the problems that matter to the self-actualizing person. Thus, over and above the attitudinal stance toward life assumed by the self-actualizing person, we find his or her functionality dominated by the emotional, interpersonal, and intellectual dimensions.

Still, the heart of Maslow's contribution appears to be motivational. He does not really emphasize the ongoing contribution of physical dimensions such as fitness to the energy reservoir of the fully functioning person (although he does, to be sure, speak to the satisfaction of basic physiological or survival needs as a necessary condition of self actualization). While he emphasizes the emotional-interpersonal realm, he does not really give us the operational ingredients that would serve to expand our humanity. Finally, while he implicitly and explicitly deals with the role of the intellect, he does not break out the technological skills of the content, learning, and teaching activities of fully functioning people.

What Maslow does give us is an extraordinarily clear vision of the developmental stages of the motivational levels that guide an individual toward self-actualization. Those people assuming physiological survival may aspire to the level of incentives that would insure their safety and security at one level and facilitate their belonging and affiliation at the next level. Those persons who have conquered the external rewards and punishments of the incentive level can aspire to the internalized rewards of the level of self-esteem and achievement. Those persons who have satisfied their achievement motives may aspire to actualize themselves within the life space they have available to them. Finally, in their increasing interdependency, those persons who are actualizing themselves expand their life space to incorporate dimensions of missions gathered from the frames of reference of those with whom they interrelate. They find missions outside of themselves and, in so doing, they find themselves.

In conclusion, the heart of Maslow's contribution is the motivational factor. In any ultimate equation accounting for actualizing human potential, the motivational factor is the catalyst that energizes the interpersonal and intellectual factors to mobilize and make these contributions. Maslow has taught us where humankind begins to actualize its potential. It remains for us to understand where humankind culminates its potential.

REFERENCES

Maslow, A. H. *Religion, Values and Peak Experiences.* Columbus: Ohio State University Press, 1964.
———. *Toward a Psychology of Being.* New York: Van Nostrand Reinhold, 1968.
———. *Motivation and Personality.* New York: Harper and Row, 1970.
———. *The Farther Reaches of Human Nature.* New York: Penguin Books, 1972.

III
Toward understanding actualizing

4
Some dimensions
of actualizing

*Many years ago, a very famous family psychological practi-
tioner, Dr. Rudolph Dreikurs, was having a lengthy and intense
debate with a behavioristic colleague about freedom and determinism. Exhausted, Dr. Dreikurs turned and asked for my
intervention. I replied: "I believe that a person who believes he is
free is free and a person who believes he is determined is
determined."*

Perhaps the main characteristic distinguishing fully functioning
people from all other people is this experience of freedom. All other
people are manipulated by force of circumstances to do things—
independent of any set of values. The best of them know why they
are doing the things. The least of them do not. They just do. Indeed,
some have made a fetish out of their determinism by doing so-called
market research on everything they are to do. Otherwise, they would
not know what they are determined by force of circumstances to do.
They are truly determined.

People moving toward actualizing themselves have a sense of purpose and their initiatives are based upon that purpose. They develop their personal programs to achieve and expand that purpose. To be sure, a critical part of their programs is to be open to input from all people who will affect or who will be affected by their initiatives. However, this input, as all other input, will be processed by fully functioning people to determine their own personalized courses of action. They are free.

My studies of actualizing human potential have led me to understand the meaning of freedom for the fully functioning person and, conversely, the meaning of determinism for the less-than-fully functioning person. Freedom and spontaneity are found in the response repertoire of the fully functioning person. It is, simply stated, not just mathematically greater in quantity but geometrically greater in quality than those of others. The power of the response repertoire comes from its continual expansion as well as from its constant multiplication in permutations and combinations.

Let us draw an illustration from the interpersonal arena. Most people—by far the vast majority of spouses, parents, teachers, helpers, and employers—never make one response in their entire lives that is accurately responsive to the expressions of other people. First of all, they do not know how to listen, so they do not "hear." Secondly, they do not know how to communicate. They may say warm and loving things that communicate their love ("I love you"). But real love is communicated through understanding and they simply do not have the responses in their repertoire to respond accurately to others.

Fully functioning people never have a conversation with anyone in which they do not "hear" the other person's expression. Where it is a task-oriented conversation, they will communicate accurately the content of the expression by others. Where it is an affective-oriented conversation, they will communicate accurately the feeling and the meaning of the expression. When it is appropriate they will go on to personalize problems and goals and individualize courses of action and programs to implement them. They have all of these degrees of flexibility because they have the responses in their repertoire.

The difference between fully and less-than-fully functioning people can be seen most clearly in a simple study conducted by Dr. David N. Aspy of the National Consortium for Humanizing Education (1978). He gave three cards to third-grade teachers of reading. On each card was written a feeling word: happy, sad, and angry. The teachers were instructed to use one of these feeling words after each student recitation. Accordingly, they responded:

"You feel happy because you got all the words right."

"You feel sad because you still can't get those words."

"You feel angry because you know you can do better."

The students gained dramatically in their reading achievement over the next year. "How," you might ask, "can this be since all teachers are taught the importance of empathy?" The answer is simple: They were not taught the skills involved; they had only the concepts and did not know how to implement them. To sum, they did not have the responses in their interpersonal skills repertoire.

Perhaps you can recall your third-grade experience. You sit in a small circle. You are a member of one of the reading groups. The teacher sits with you as each of you in turn recites. You are a bit apprehensive as the teacher looks to you. The teacher says, "Next!" and it is your turn. You start a little shakey but gradually you gain confidence. At the end you are quite happy—even proud with your performance. You look to the teacher with anticipation. Do you remember what the teacher said?

"Next!"

In spite of an understanding of the concept of empathy; in spite of the best intentions in the world, the teacher could offer only the responses she had in her repertoire. And she did not have responses for responding accurately. Because she never learned those responses.

The effective ingredients of freedom are the responses in one's repertoire. The fully functioning people I have observed and inventoried are constantly seeking to expand that response repertoire as the source of their freedom as well as their productivity and creativity.

As was demonstrated most clearly in the preceding illustration: a person is not free to respond to others if he or she does not have the responses with which to respond. An individual cannot make discriminations about where and when to make certain responses if he or she does not have the responses available. We can "free" the slaves but leave them entrapped within their bodies, souls, and minds if they are not taught or they do not learn the responses necessary to exercise freedom. A person can express himself or herself haphazardly on a paint canvas, but is not free because he or she does not know the basic brush strokes and cannot make free discriminations about how and when and where to apply them. We are trapped by our own limited responses.

FULLY FUNCTIONING PEOPLE

We know something about fully functioning and less-than-fully functioning people from existing research on developing human resources (Carkhuff and Berenson, 1967, 1977). We can see these two groups of people most clearly over a period of crises. Fully functioning people grow with each crisis and their resolution of the last crisis serves to diminish the dimensions of the next crisis. Less-than-fully functioning people deteriorate with each crisis and their inability to manage the last crisis contributes directly to the next crisis.

Fully functioning people consider crises as opportunities for them and others to grow. They mobilize their resources and intensify their efforts at the crisis points. They exercise their cumulating responses in new combinations tailored to the particular interaction of factors involved. In short, they exercise their freedom.

In contrast, less-than-fully functioning people are overpowered by crises. They function best when conditions are best—at the beginning of a relationship, learning, or a job. Teachers, for example, function at their highest levels on the first day of school in their first year of teaching. They never recover fully from the first mid-school-year crisis (around the Christmas season). And they repeat this experience year after year until they have extinguished their functionality (Aspy and Roebuck, 1978).

If we think of life as a series of crises—crises at home, in school, at work, in the community—then we can understand the differences most clearly. Fully functioning people live their lives in preparation for crises. Fully functioning people are most energetic and vital and resourceful in crisis. They come alive in crisis. Less-than-fully functioning people live, relatively speaking, most fully in the "filler," seeking only to avoid the crises that they stimulate by their lack of openness and preparation.

Indeed, there is evidence to suggest that fully functioning people are not only quantitatively, but also qualitatively, different from less-than-fully functioning people (Berenson and Mitchell, 1974). They do quantitatively more of the things that others do; they also do the things significantly better. Thus, for example, in helping others at crises points in their lives, fully functioning people will respond more accurately and initiate more effectively. Less-than-fully functioning people will not even attend effectively to others, because they will be caught up in conflicting personal implications of the crises of others for themselves.

The effects of the efforts of fully functioning people are dramatic (Carkhuff and Berenson, 1967, 1977). With intensive and extensive experiences, brought on by repeated crises, people move in the direction of their level of functioning. In one study of the effects of counseling, the helpee of the helper functioning at the highest levels of helping was functioning, subsequent to counseling, at levels of helping higher than all other helpers in the study. Thus, with time and intimate exposure to the fully functioning person, other people tend to function in similar ways. Fully functioning people tend to affect the people around them in growing waves of concentric circles. To know them is to grow with them.

Not only are they more productive with people-products, fully functioning people are more productive with all kinds of products. They have a history of tangible accomplishments and high performance indicators in a variety of areas, including public recognition of leadership and productivity. Thus, if they are teachers, they gain teaching and research awards and develop materials about their work that they share with others. If they are business people, they can demonstrate management efficiency and product profitability. Likewise, if they are in government, they can demonstrate the costs and benefits of the accomplishments of their different services or products. Let us look at the dimensions that lead to their enormous productivity.

DIMENSIONS OF ACTUALIZATION

In my study of people actualizing human potential, I observed and interviewed many hundreds of people in ongoing research. Of these, seven originally qualified as people moving toward actualization. The ways in which they converged with each other and contrasted with others will be elaborated later in the text.

Of the seven self-actualizing people or actualizers studied, none were famous in the respect of being public figures who would be recognized nationally or internationally—although they were prominent within their speciality areas. (This may or may not say something about the exclusiveness of the attraction and the demands of public recognition and the actualizing of human potential.) Five were men and one was a minority group member, again facts that remain to be explicated. Two were in business and industry; three in government and association work; and two were in teaching or human services.

All were over thirty-five years of age, with two of the seven being in their late thirties; two being in their forties; and three being in their fifties. It is anticipated that above a certain minimum age, there is no relationship between actualization and age. Evidence from other areas suggests that more than 99% of professionals never make a significant contribution beyond their early thirties. Thirty-five seems like a good cut-off age to insure that the individual has demonstrated a continuous track record of productivity and, implicitly, crisis management. We did not, like Maslow, study college students or ask them about their "peak" experiences (there is usually only one kind for them). Rather, we have suggested a reversal of the youthful wisdom of the 1960s: "Never trust a person under thirty-five. The first part of life is a 'free-ride.'" The story of the actualization of human potential is told over years of functioning.

In terms of productivity, all self-actualizing people we studied had been recipients at one point or another of awards such as "Man of the Year" or "Woman of the Year" awards, research awards, teaching awards, and association awards. Collectively, they had written more than thirty books and acquired any number of copyrights, patents, trademarks, and other indices of accomplishment, with each having contributed to these totals. All had held important leadership roles at different points in their lives and this has been reflected in their educational and career development and public recognition.

Fortunately for us, our actualizers found people in their environments who were both models and agents for their growth and development. To be sure, the actualizers found an average of seven people who had a significant impact upon their growth and development. In contrast, non-actualizers indicated approximately three facilitators in their life experience. All of the actualizers and few of the non-actualizers indicated one or more of their parents as a significant source of effect upon their development. Further, the actualizers experienced fewer retarders (2) than the non-actualizers (4). Whether the actualizers found the helpers or the helpers produced the actualizers is a question. We suspect that it is an interaction of both sources, especially after the person has had the initial facilitative experiences. The sources of growth and development will be considered further in later sections of this work.

In this context, the basic assumptions people make about life did not seem to be a discriminating item. While all of the actualizers made some assumptions about growing, so did some of the non-actualizers. Perhaps it just seemed like the right thing to do for the non-actualizers. In any event, the actualizers lived growing while the non-actualizers talked growing. Clearly, the assumptions we make about life are necessary but not sufficient conditions of life. The life assumptions actualizers make, as well as their implications, will be considered further later.

What did appear to be discriminating among the actualizers and the non-actualizers is an experience that we will call *marginality*. Perhaps it is redundant to say that actualizers are marginal people. Whether or not they are comfortable economically, they experience themselves and others experience them as "different." Life on the margin leads to different perspectives and, thus, greater creativity than life with people who are "mainstreamed."

In this regard, actualizers are not necessarily rewarded for their creativity and productivity. Indeed, they recognize fully that the rewards and punishments they receive are independent of the contributions they have made. Thus, for any single effort they are as likely to be punished as they are to be rewarded. For them, it is like living in the land of the blind: The non-actualizers say that if the actualizers will only remove those two strange bumps under their foreheads, they would be eminently more acceptable. The reactions and the liabilities of functioning fully will be detailed later.

The true discriminating dimensions occur in the inventorying of the physical, emotional, and intellectual functioning of the actualizers. The actualizers differ in substantial ways from the non-actualizers on these dimensions.

Physical functioning

The physical dimension is the least discriminating of these dimensions, only because it is in vogue now to maintain some kind of a fitness program. In any event, all actualizers maintain rigorous fitness programs. However, they do not make a fetish out of it. I am reminded of some of the non-actualizers who run two hours or more every day and then are unable to do anything else. The real question for the actualizers is: Fitness for what? They draw upon their physical resources to serve other more important purposes in their lives. They value their fitness highly because they recognize it as a necessary but not sufficient condition of their life purpose. Interestingly, all the actualizers I observed tend to be slightly overweight, thus seeming to draw upon these reserves in the service of their purposes. In addition, while they are healthy, they have suffered an assortment of illnesses, including heart surgery, sugar diabetes, and other illnesses. However, these illnesses appear to present only temporary set-backs in their movement toward their goals. Indeed, as with all other crises, actualizers treat health crises as opportunities to learn more about themselves and others.

Emotional functioning

There seem to be two critical emotional factors. Both have motivational translations. We may, if we wish, call these "emotivational" factors. The first of these is personal or intrapersonal; that is, occurring within the person. For actualizers, the intrapersonal emotivation comes down squarely on the development of missions outside of themselves. These missions typically involve causes of justice for specific subpopulations such as women, minorities, and children. In this context, they tend to emphasize education and government services to achieve their missions. For non-actualizers, the mission never gets outside of themselves. At best, it is their own personal career development. Every mission statement by every leader is seen by the non-actualizers in the context of the implications for their own personal career development. At worst, they fall outside of the incentives that motivate a person to develop a career.

The second emotional factor is an extension of the first. In a sense, emotivation involves committing oneself to someone else's mission. This means entering another person's frame of reference and tuning in on his or her experience. It means learning the things that matter to someone else. All actualizers have the skills to respond accurately to another person's experience. No non-actualizers have accurate responsive skills. Thus, they are precluded from expanding the boundaries of their humanity. For the interpersonal dimension, emotivation serves the function of expanding the size of the individual and what he or she stands for in life.

Intellectual functioning

There are three primary intellectual factors that discriminate actualizers from non-actualizers. The first of these is a person's substantive specialty or area of professional or technical expertise. The thing that discriminates actualizers from non-actualizers is degree of expertise. Actualizers can operationalize *any* goal in their specialty area and develop the necessary systems and technologies to achieve it. That is what makes them truly professional. Non-actualizers usually have only the facts and concepts. Their basic nonsubstantive principle is to "learn the language." In those few instances where they learn a principle or a skill (always from actualizers as the source), they parade it for a lifetime as if they did, indeed, know what they were doing.

The second intellectual factor involves learning. Succinctly, actualizers are always learning. No matter how they pretend, non-actualizers are never learning. Where actualizers hook themselves up in a self-sustaining and recycling, life-long learning process, non-actualizers become specialists. Their favorite mode is to explore an area. They become experts in what the educators term and themselves represent—divergent production. To be sure, they get all of the publicity up front on a project because no one knows better than they that the project will never culminate in human benefits.

Finally, the third intellectual factor involves teaching. Actualizers see communicating their learnings to others as part of their personal and/or professional responsibilities. In addition, they recognize the interactional benefits of teaching and learning for their own personal learning. Accordingly, actualizers incorporate all of the ingredients of effective teaching to develop and deliver their content. Non-actualizers never teach except in an authoritarian, didactic, highly verbal, lowly experiential mode. Because they are never teaching what they know, they are never learning what they do not know.

In summary, actualizers are separated from non-actualizers by their physical, emotional, and intellectual functioning. It is these factors, alone and in their various interactions, that make the actualizers so much more powerful in their productivity and in the actualization process that leads to that productivity. Given their combinations and permutations of responses, at any given point in time, especially at the crises points of life, they have 360° of freedom.

Actualizers experience this freedom. Some experience themselves as independent of the rest of their world (see Figure 4-1). It is as if they conceive of "Real Life" (actualizing human potential in self and others) as independent of "Apparent Life" (that which others call the "real world"). Life stands as a truth in relation to a mix of truths and myths (the real world requires at least some truth to perpetuate itself). The task of life is to separate out the truth from the myth and to stand with the truth.

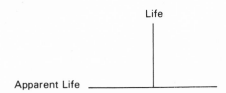

Figure 4-1   The independent dimensions of life and apparent life

The person who stands as a truth among the mix of truth and myth is an actualized person—separated from others by energy and emotivational supports and intellectual deliveries. The others are determined: They are trapped by lower-class survival needs or middle-class comforts or upper-class luxuries in roles that drain their vital energies, motives, and acuity.

Who believes he is free and skilled to implement that freedom is free. Who either believes he is determined or is unskilled to implement freedom is determined.

REFERENCES

Aspy, D. N. and Roebuck, F. N. *KIDS*. Amherst, Mass.: Human Resource Development Press, 1978.

Berenson, B. G. and Mitchell, K. *Confrontation in Counseling and Life*. Amherst, Mass.: Human Resource Development Press, 1973.

Carkhuff, R. R. and Berenson, B. G. *Beyond Counseling and Therapy*. New York: Holt, Rinehart and Winston, 1967, 1977.

5
Some sources
of actualizing

*A number of years ago we conducted research assessing the
effects of high-, moderate-, and low-functioning helpers upon
high-, moderate-, and low-functioning helpees. The basic experimental manipulation was to present either the helpers or helpees
with crises in the helping process. Thus, for the helper, we
manipulated the degree to which the helpees would explore
themselves in a helping situation: the helpees explored themselves at high levels during the first-third of the session; lowered
their levels of self-exploration by becoming impersonal,
irrelevant, and distant during the middle-third; and again raised
their levels of functioning during the last-third. We studied the
helper's level of helping skills offered during these three periods.
What we found was very revealing.*

*The low-level functioning helpers deteriorated severely in
their helping skills during the middle-third and regressed to a
totally uninvolved and unskilled level from which they never
recovered. The moderate-functioning helpers deteriorated, but not
as severely, and improved, but never again to their previous*

level. The high-level functioning helpers intensified and elevated their levels of functioning during the experimental period and never again returned to their previous levels.

A composite description of the low-functioning helpers was compiled by the helpees (Carkhuff and Berenson, 1967, 1977):

> *A composite of the low-rated helper shows an unimaginative, uncreative, boring, and pedestrian person. He performs his function in a mechanical, perfunctory manner, never expressing any emotion, and doesn't respond to the feelings expressed. The tenacity of these helpers not to get involved with anything human was frightening. They seemed to be comfortable only in a safe, neutral range. This often was evidenced by the questions asked— detailed information communicating surface values such as societal status, financial means, and other unimportant details. His questions didn't communicate respect. One showed a complete lack of concern for me until his questions revealed my financial status. Then his voice showed life for the first time as if then I was worth paying attention to. I was really disgusted.*
>
> *With more frequency than I found tolerable, there was a lot of sick kind of giggling and I didn't think my problem was all that funny (and I know that he did not understand the experimental purposes of my session). I struggled desperately to get something out of him and couldn't. I could handle him on his level but I couldn't bring him up to mine. My lack of respect for him showed in my responses to his questions. During the middle section I found it not only easy but sadistically pleasurable to manipulate him, for within the first five minutes I found myself unable to feel any respect for him. I felt most comfortable talking chit-chat with these people as opposed to the internal struggle experienced with the more facilitative helpers.*
>
> *His "blah" voice and lack of reaction dragged me down. I couldn't reach out and grab anything because it's just a mask with words coming out. He made me feel as if I, as a client, was some kind of animal, and he couldn't go down to the client's feelings or he'd just get soiled. What he was really saying to me was "I am worthless, empty, sterile, nothing, only I have learned to keep this from the world and you. In intimacy with you, you bring me back to who I really am and you get me dirty again."*
>
> *I knew this ineffectual didn't know and couldn't ever know me. I would have erased him from my memory except for purposes of this study, as an interesting example of destructive therapy. I invariably left depressed from sessions with these people.*

As can be seen, the low-level helpers had severely restricted repertoires of responses that disabled them immediately and permanently. They were able to gain no new insights and develop no new action programs to cope with the crisis situation. They were incapable of performing in the helping role.

A composite description of the moderate-level functioning helpers follows:

> *A composite picture of the helper who was neither facilitator nor retarder gives no vitality or life. He accepts weakness where I keep trying to show my strength. He is so depressed in manner and voice that I need to cheer him up. His technique is to let you know he's weak and can't help. He's very polite and so sorry but he has his own needs, so that you end up feeling compassion and start working around his needs. The dominant feeling the client goes away with is that this guy must be left unhurt and unharmed so you have to be very careful and not get into anything that might disturb his equilibrium. He tunes in on your strength and asks you for it.*
>
> *There are lots of quips and smiles to show what a great guy or gal the helper is. He asks many factual questions, shallow, bright but often leading to obtuse answers. He laughs too much. I say I'm practically psychotic over this picture and he laughs. He is happy during the middle section when he can talk superficially about himself. It's the middle part when I'm tapping in on who the helper really is. He can be active now. He thinks I'm bringing the focus on him and he thinks I deserve something from him. I stirred up a reservoir of guilt for not acting before. As soon as he spills some shallow emotion, he is able to maintain his former equilibrium, the only place where he feels safe.*
>
> *The middle-range people can listen with a bare minimum of respect and make some effort to treat you as a kind of human, but they are unable to carry you for any length of time and usually find a way to get you to carry them. Often these people can sympathize and give you the feeling that we're just two frail people huddled together in this cruel, cold world and I'll comfort you and you comfort me and somehow we'll survive. But they cannot show you how to stand up and fight or try to go beyond this point, and probably don't want to see anyone able to go beyond the point at which they themselves are stuck. These helpers never recoup fully after the middle section.*

As well he noted, the moderate helpers managed to stay within their roles outside of the crisis, even recovering somewhat after the crisis. However, they evidenced no new insights or programs to cope with the crisis. They simply functioned well in the helping role in noncrisis situations. Unfortunately, helping deals with crisis situations.

A composite of the high-functioning helpers follows:

*The composite high-rated helper is an exciting, stimulating, intel-
ligent, creative, exploring adventurous person. He offers life. It's
like the air he breathes. He is really only being what he has to be.
He is living himself.*

*He gives me new concepts rather than merely parroting mine.
He helps me to see places to go. He gave me the impression of a
genuine commitment to an interpersonal encounter. He seemed to
be experiencing it rather than intellectually following. He is with
you and will fight for your life with you. That's the comfort of him.
He is siding with the constructive forces in you. He will add his
100% to your 20% that's constructive. His analogies and con-
creteness are such that you don't have to ponder about what he
means—you immediately understand intellectually and simultaneously feel it as never before.*

*During the middle section I had a real internal struggle to pull
myself away from reality and involvement so that I could complete
the experiment. With these people, it hurt me to try to manipulate
them, as if they deserved more respect from me. During the experimental period, manipulation, the high-rated helper starts
grabbing to keep you from falling away. He plunges in and
becomes more intense.*

*I never needed to take notes afterwards on my impressions of
high-rated helpers because I knew that I could never forget the
encounter. His intensity made me feel like throwing myself into his
arms, and that I could trust his holding. I could feel him peeling
away the layers. He wanted my deepest feelings and I felt he
respected them. He always left me feeling more hopeful and more
courageous. I knew that he knew a lot about me and that he could
really someday come to know me.*

*The high-functioning helpers had an extensive repertoire of
responses that enabled them to intensify their efforts. They
developed new insights and new actions to cope with the crisis.
They rose above their roles to become fully human in the crisis.
They recognized that the meat of life—the opportunities to grow
or deteriorate—occur in the crisis.*

*The results were similar for the helpees in studies experi-
mentally manipulating the helpers' levels of functioning. For
these studies the experimental manipulation was the helper's
shift to impersonal, irrelevant, and distant communications from
his previous levels, whether high, moderate, or low. We studied
the helpee's level of exploration with similar results. In a role
reversal, the high-functioning helpees mobilized and intensified
their efforts, carrying on to help their helpers catch up again
with them. The moderate-functioning helpees explored*

*themselves more or less as a function of their helpers. The low-
functioning helpees deteriorated in functioning and never again
recovered.*

The results of this research gave us some profound insights into the
effects of crises upon people functioning at different levels. Most
never recover from the first crisis. Some recover slightly. A very few
get vitalized at its presentation. The discriminating function is the
ability to incorporate the data in the moment and develop insights
based upon the data and programs based upon the insights. High-
functioning helpers can do this. Low- and moderate-functioning
can not.

In the end, there is no real difference between moderate- and
low-level functioning people. Low functioning is simply a more advanced state of deterioration. Both are qualitatively different from
the fully functioning person.

INSIGHT AND ACTION

Perhaps the most important ability of actualizers is their ability to
develop insights and action programs in their lives and in the lives
of those around them. What all actualizers comprehend is the need
to systematically develop their insights from as many sources as
they can find (needs assessments) and to systematically develop the
action programs that flow from these insights (planning). While
some non-actualizers understand the need for insights, in practice
they do not develop the insights systematically. Although other non-
actualizers recognize the importance of action programs, and in
practice develop the programs systematically, they do so from very
limited insights. None of the non-actualizers develop both insights
and actions systematically.

This ability to develop both insights and action means simply
that the fully functioning person has an extensive repertoire of responses for doing so. Actualizers know how to elicit input from all
sources potentially affecting or being affected by their programs.
They know how to respond to input to facilitate its further exploration from an internal frame of reference. They know how to diagnose
input in terms of its level of functioning within the parameters
delineated. They know how to personalize input in terms of problems
and, more importantly, in terms of the goals that flow from both the

internal and external frames of reference. All of these activities culminate in data-based planning for the individual or the group that he or she is leading.

What the individual does with that insight is as important as developing the insight. Because actualizers have developed their insights systematically, their programs flow directly from the insights. Indeed, the more data upon which the insights are based, the more clearly they point to the goals; the more clear the goals are, the more systematically they can develop their programs. Thus, actualizers become engaged in all of the activities that make their programs work—operationalizing their goals in behavioral terms; developing their systems of delivering or achieving the goals in comprehensive designs; developing their deliveries in atomistic detail; making their deliveries in integrated processes; and shaping new and more accurate insights with the data from the feedback of the action program, thereby promising more effective action programs in the future.

What, you may ask, are the insights and actions upon which the development of actualized people is based? In other words, what are the sources of effect in actualizing human potential? There are many sources of this ability of actualizers to systematically develop insights and action programs.

Modeling

Perhaps the most significant source of human development is modeling or imitation. If the helper or modeler can become a potent influencer for the helpee or learner, the effects can be dramatic. Such a helper can become the source of insights and action and, what is more important, the direct source of behavioral repertoires (Bandura, 1969). The focus of interest is upon the helper's intentional or unintentional performance of complex behavioral patterns that may be imitated and adapted by the helpee or learner.

All of the actualizers studied indicated their parents were the initial source of learning for actualizing their potential. In all but one instance, they indicated their parents to be among the most potent influencers of their behavior. While many of the non-actualizers respected the contributions of their parents, it is clear that the effects were not nearly so impactful. Most significant, the actualizers indicated that the facilitative experience their parents gave them enabled them to discriminate between the facilitators and the

retarders in their daily experiences. Thus, they ⎜
both the number of facilitators as well as the contr
people. At the same time, they could minimize the
detractions of the retarders.

Expectancies

One of the ways that potent reinforcers influence the development of
effective insight and action behavior on the part of their helpees or
learners is through their expectancies or expectations. Expectancies
on the part of significant authority figures lead to learner behavior
that is congruent with those expectancies (Clark, 1965; Rosenthal
and Jacobson, 1968). Thus, helpers whose expectations for a given
learner or group of learners are high elicit constructive change or
gain, whereas helpers whose expectations for the learners are low
have retarding effects upon the behaviors of the learners. In short,
learners come to expect of themselves what their potent reinforcers
have expected of them.

All of the actualizers indicated high expectancies of them, initially by their parents and then by a succession of facilitative agents
throughout their lives. Some of the non-actualizers reported overly
high expectancies that were unrelated to planning and programming functions and thus unachievable. The result was that they
have considered themselves failures, no matter what their achievements. Most indicated no initially high or continuously high expectancies. Rather, they recalled sermons such as admonishments to
"not get into trouble" as the modal experience. So, the accuracy of
the expectancies is critical. For the actualizers, the potent reinforcers seemed to ask of them neither more nor less than they could
handle in their planning and programming activities. For the non-
actualizers, people seemed constantly to be asking more and/or less
than they were capable.

Participation

One of the things that the potent reinforcers do with the aspiring
actualizers is involve them in the process leading to their own expectancies. In other words, as one of the persons being affected by
the outcomes and, thus, possibly affecting the outcomes, the learner
has the opportunity to provide his or her input. Thus, the helpers, in

developing their own insights, receive input from the helpees. The authority figures of very few non-actualizers receive input from the helpees and, when they do, they tend to be overpowered by it in a child-centered or student-centered abdication of their responsibilities.

At a minimum, participation increases motivation and personal satisfaction (Lewin, 1951). At a maximum, increased motivation may lead to increased performance. Thus, the actualizers studied had the experience of an integration of the modeling and expectancy sources of learning in their participatory experience. The helpers modeled how they developed the insights upon which the expectancies they had for the helpees were based. At the same time, the helpees had the experience of self-potency by participating in formulating their own destinies. The non-actualizers had no such integrative experience.

Reinforcement

Perhaps the most powerful tool available to humans for learning new behaviors is the selective or differential reinforcement of responses. Most human behavior is produced and maintained by the contingencies of reinforcement existing in everyday life. For the layman, the concept of differential reinforcement may translate simply into a system of rewards and punishments: Constructive or goal-directed behavior is rewarded; destructive behavior is punished; neutral behavior is observed vigilantly to determine whether the behavior is constructive or destructive.

For the actualizers and the non-actualizers in our study the experiences of reinforcement were very different. For the actualizers, reinforcements were developmental, consistent, and appropriate to their frames of reference—first, unconditional to produce any behavior at all; then positive to reinforce constructive behavior; later positive, neutral, and negative to influence constructive behavior and extinguish destructive behavior; and, finally, conditional for constructive behavior as the expectancies were established firmly. For the non-actualizers, the reinforcers were inconsistently applied—primarily neutral (ignoring) and/or punishment for failure to achieve inappropriate goals that were unrelated to their frames of reference.

All of these sources of growth and development are integrated in a healthy learning experience: The helper models the behaviors being taught didactically and learned experientially; the expectancies the helper has for the helpee are high but accurate (within the grasp of the helpee); the helpee participates as a source in the development of both the insights and the behaviors and, thus, is motivated to learn the responses; the helpee is differentially reinforced according to his or her demonstrated ability to move toward growth. Of course, all of these sources of growth are predicated upon the effectiveness with which they are employed by the helper as well as the effectiveness that the helpee discovers in applying the self same sources in his or her own life. In addition, all of the sources of growth are contingent upon the helper's development as a potent person for the helpee.

Who, then, must the helper be to become a potent model, guide, agent, and reinforcer for the helpee? The effective helper must become all of the things that the actualizer later demonstrates in his or her life. The effective helper must develop a high energy level that enables him or her to be strongest at the crises of life; a high level of motivation to accomplish a mission that directs and sustains him or her throughout life; a high level of responsiveness that enables him or her to expand the boundaries of his or her humanity to incorporate the missions of others; a high degree of expertise in his or her substantive specialty that enables him or her to make contributions in life; a highly skilled learning disposition that enables him or her to engage in a life-long learning process; a highly skilled teaching disposition that enables him or her to communicate learnings and contributions to others and so, to learn from the feedback they provide. In other words, the potent helper must be a fully functioning person.

What, then, must the helper *do* to become a potent model, guide, agent, and reinforcer for the helpee? First, the helper, as we have indicated, must *be* or represent whatever he or she is offering. Second, the helper must enter the helpee's frame of reference to hook that frame of reference up with learning goals that are instrumental for the helpee's purposes. Third, the helper must be able to develop programs that insure the helpee's successful and progressive movement from where the helpee is to the goal.

Another way of saying this is to say that the helper must have both responsive and initiative skills—responsive skills to enter the learner's frame of reference; initiative skills to take the learners from where they are to where they want or need to be. The responsive and initiative dimensions are directly related to the insight and action dimensions with which we began our exploration. The responsive dimensions facilitate the development of accurate insights. The initiative dimensions stimulate the development of effective action. Together, the responsive and initiative dimensions represent what it is the effective helpers are really offering—movement toward life.

There is a schematic way of representing these dimensions (see Figure 5-1). As can be seen the responsive and initiative factors can be represented on a continuum: The responsive ranges from sensitivity to insensitivity or nonresponsiveness; the initiative ranges from action orientation to passivity or noninitiative. In addition, there is evidence to indicate that these dimensions are independent of each other. Here, we have represented this orthogonality by having them bisect each other at right angles (Berenson and Mitchell, 1973). For all of this we have evidence.

For the constructs, we do not have empirical evidence. But we do have experiential evidence. Typically, society conditions its females to function in feminine roles. However, whether or not the persons involved are males or females, these roles range between being responsive and passive. The conditioned woman, at her most functional, is a nurturant person—warm and sensitive, and receptive. At least functional, she is passive and detractive or subtractive from others.

Typically, society conditions its males to function in masculine roles. These roles range between being initiative and insensitive. The conditioned man, at his most functional, is a strong person—directionful and action-oriented and initiative. At worst, he is insensitive and destructive.

It is to be emphasized that these constructs represent societal conditioning of roles rather than the inherent response dispositions of either the males or the females being conditioned. Obviously, both

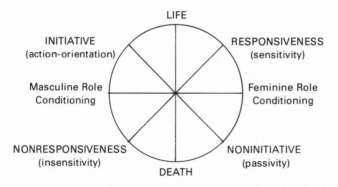

Figure 5-1   Some constructs bisecting the responsive and initiative factors of human development

males and females can be both responsive and initiative, or for that matter both can be, as the great majority are, nonresponsive and noninitiative.

And that is just the point, for it is postulated that life bisects the responsive and initiative dimensions. Indeed, we cannot be truly responsive if we are not also highly initiative. Vice versa, we cannot be truly initiative if we are also not highly responsive. There is no accurate understanding without action just as there is no effective action without understanding. To be sure, we cannot achieve the heights of either responsiveness or initiative without converging both of them. We cannot be fully alive without developing our responsiveness and initiative at higher and higher levels.

Conversely, death bisects nonresponsiveness and noninitiative. The dying person is insensitive and passive, which is precisely why it is so difficult to react to him or her and thus dissociate oneself. It is also precisely why people who are dying—physically, emotionally, and intellectually—are able to take so many people with them. They are so subtle in subtracting from the people around them. It is like taking a gram of food or energy away each minute or hour or day so that in eighteen years, seventy-six days, five hours, and twenty-six minutes, a person starves to death.

Clearly, one can plot all of the people, organizations, and orientations he or she encounters in life according to their degree of responsiveness and initiative—according to whether they are moving toward life or death, with that movement having direct implications for the movement of the people around them.

Once again, the theme of previous chapters emerges: Life and Apparent Life are independent of one another. In Apparent Life, the human dimensions are funneled into roles and the human mentality is conditioned by threats and punishments. There are people living inside these roles. Some are even proud of having maintained a core of human integrity, however small and shriveled. These people relate role-to-role. They think, feel, and act only within the very precise definitions of their roles. When they cross the boundaries of these roles, they are no longer trustworthy for society and they are banished.

In Life, the human dimensions converge and are funneled into increasingly responsive initiatives (or initiative responses), they reach to heights unknown before. They not only break with their roles but with their limits in a spiraling, elevating evolution to fulfill themselves and, in so doing, humankind. They relate soul-to-soul and leave larger for the experience. They think, feel, and act the thoughts, feelings, and actions reserved in our fantasies only for the gods. Indeed, every moment for them is a peak experience because they are living fully and fulfilling themselves in it.

To sum, actualizers are moving toward the fulfillment of themselves and those around them who choose likewise; just as they, themselves, were yielded by intimate contacts with people struggling to provide themselves and others with opportunities to fulfill themselves. It is critical for actualizers to pass the experience of freedom and the assignment of its responsibility from one generation to the next. If only one person in each generation actualizes his or her human potential, it is enough to rationalize the existence of humanity.

REFERENCES

Bandura, A. "Behavioral modification through modeling procedures." In L. Krasner and L. P. Ullmann (Eds.), *Research in Behavior Modification: New Developments and Implications*. New York: Holt, Rinehart and Winston, 1965.

Berenson, B. G. and Mitchell, K. *Confrontation in Counseling and Life*. Amherst, Mass.: Human Resource Development Press, 1973.

Carkhuff, R. R. and Berenson, B. G. *Beyond Counseling and Therapy*. New York: Holt, Rinehart and Winston, 1967, 1977.

Clark, K. The effects of prejudice and discrimination on personality development. *Proceedings Mid-Century White House Conference*, 1950.

Lewin, K. *Field Theory in Social Science*. New York: Harper and Row, 1951.

Rosenthal, R. and Jacobson, L. *Pygmalion in the Classroom: Teacher Expectation and Pupils' Intellectual Development*. New York: Holt, Rinehart and Winston, 1968.

IV
Toward operationalizing actualizing

6
Toward measuring actualizing

In 1979 I recall teaching human and community resource development at an international conclave of Jesuit priests at the ancient Gregorian University in Rome. One of the Eastern priests gave as an example of actualization of human potential the case of a monk who sat high in the mountains communicating with God. My response was, "That's immoral!" It is immoral to be blessed with an intellect that can raise our human condition and not to use it. It is immoral to be blessed with the ability to right the wrongs of the existing human condition and to do nothing to improve them. It is immoral to retreat, in the face of our human problems, to the privatization of motives that now dominate our society when we have the intelligence to address human goals of our own making.

It is one thing to postulate a model for actualizing human potential. It is quite another to measure it. Yet, measurement is precisely what we must be able to do. We must measure not simply because it is dictated by the use of logic and the scientific method that we describe, predict, and control our worlds. If we cannot measure human potential, we cannot operationalize our goals for actualizing it; therefore, we cannot develop programs to achieve it.

In the following measurement efforts the dimensions of human potential are summarized as physical, emotional, and intellectual factors. The emotional includes personal motivational and interpersonal dimensions. The intellectual includes substantive, learning, and teaching dimensions.

PHYSICAL FACTORS

The first of the factors of human potential is a physical factor. The physical factor includes the dimensions of cardiorespiratory functioning, endurance, strength, and flexibility as well as the rest and nutrition needed to support fitness (see Table 6-1). There are a number of ways that we can measure fitness for our purposes. One way is to observe behavior over a continuous period of time to determine the level at which a person functions. The other is to set up criteria based upon fitness levels. In either event, the fitness level based upon exercise will ultimately influence the fitness level of application. In other words, whatever a person's reservoir of energy ini-

TABLE 6-1 Levels of physical fitness

	Physical Functioning			
Levels of Functioning	Cardio-respiratory	Endurance	Strength	Flexibility
5 Stamina				
4 Intensity				
3 Adaptability				
2 Survival				
1 Sickness				

tially, over an extended period of time, his or her level of fitness will relate to his or her level of energy (Carkhuff, 1974; Collingwood, 1973; Collingwood and Carkhuff, 1975).

We have characterized the levels of functioning at five levels: sickness, survival, adaptability, intensity, and stamina. The scales are cumulative, with each level incorporating the previous level. Below minimally effective levels (Level 3.0), characterized by adaptability, people do not have the energy to discharge their responsibilities. They cannot mobilize to meet daily crises and, therefore, are dependent variables manipulated by forces beyond their control. Above all, they can never be trusted to be available when they are needed because they never have the energy. Above minimally effective levels, people have the fitness necessary to go on the initiative in tackling their responsibilities and their daily crises. However professional they may appear during calm times, low-functioning people are characterized by an inability to mobilize to produce when it is necessary. However calm they appear during calm times, high-functioning people are characterized by the ability to mobilize to produce when it is necessary.

Thus, at a high level (Level 5.0) of functioning stamina, individuals are able to function with stamina in terms of cardiorespiratory, endurance, strength, and flexibility indices. Such individuals can do this in all areas of functioning—at home, in education, at work, in the community. This level of functioning incorporates the intensity of the next level.

At the next highest level (Level 4.0), intensity, individuals are able to function selectively with intensity in terms of the dimensions of fitness in the different areas of functioning.

At a minimally effective level (Level 3.0), adaptability, individuals have energy sufficient to adapt to the daily requirements in the various areas of functioning. They meet the needs of all situations in which they find themselves although they may not have much left over for themselves.

At a less-than-fully functioning level (Level 2.0), survival, individuals have barely enough energy to survive each day. Such individuals are always tired and listless and unable to function effectively in any area of endeavor.

At the lowest level (Level 1.0), sickness, individuals are literally and physically sick; overpowered by even the most minimal requirements of daily existence.

The scales offered are based upon norms for males and females. They may also be modified for age and other limiting conditions. (Before checking yourself out, you should consult a physician about your overall health.) A sample of scale levels is provided in Table 6–2.

One way of checking your level of cardiorespiratory functioning is to take the step test as follows: (1) Step up onto a chair once every five seconds, for a total of twelve times within a minute; (2) Take your pulse rate for two minutes thereafter; (3) Using the appropriate norm group in Table 6–2, obtain your level of cardiorespiratory functioning. You may want some help in stepping up on to the chair so that you do not fall down. You may also want someone else to take your pulse rate.

You can do the same thing for the other indices: (1) Do the tests of endurance (how far you can walk/run in twelve minutes), strength (number of sit-ups in two minutes), and flexibility (how far you can bend down without bending your knees); (2) Look up your levels of endurance, strength, and flexibility in Table 6–2. These ratings are meant to give you a quick index of your physical functioning. A more complete picture may be developed using other sources (Collingwood and Carkhuff, 1975). Most people do relatively the best on the flexibility test and the poorest on the endurance and cardio-respiratory tests.

The modal level of functioning, or the level at which the person appears most often (use the mean or average by dividing the sum total by four if this does not occur) across the fitness dimensions constitutes an index of the person's degree of actualization of the physical dimension of human potential. Again, as for all of the following scales, this modal level may be applied in absolute terms as indicated by the norms of the scales in Table 6–2 or in relative terms related to one's own level of development and/or satisfaction.

Perhaps most important, the physical realm gives us a prototype for assessing ourselves in all other realms. While the normative data with which to compare ourselves may not be so clear in other areas of functioning, the physical realm pushes us very hard with clear-cut criteria. Either we can run a mile in six or seven minutes or we cannot. We cannot delude ourselves from day-to-day and year-to-year. Although we may feel "good" temporarily, there are long-term implications to a deteriorating physical condition for other dimensions of human potential. In the long run, we cannot actualize our human potential without the continuous support of our physical fitness and the physical energy that it serves to facilitate.

EMOTIONAL FACTORS

The emotional factors attempt to account for the push and the pull of motivation. There are at least two dominating emotional factors.

TABLE 6-2 Normative data on levels of physical fitness

PHYSICAL FUNCTIONING

Levels of Functioning	Cardiorespiratory (Pulse rate for 2 min.)		Endurance (Miles in 12 min.)		Strength (Situps in 2 min.)		Flexibility (Toe touch)
	Male	Female	Male	Female	Male	Female	Male and Female
5.0 Stamina	71	86	2.3	2.1	100	50	Palms on floor
4.5	89	95	2.0	1.9	97	35	Fists on floor
4.0 Intensity	115	120	1.8	1.7	61	27	2nd joint on floor
3.5	132	137	1.6	1.5	52	24	Fingertips on floor
3.0 Adaptability	158	163	1.5	1.4	47	20	Fingertips to toes
2.5	184	189	1.4	1.3	38	16	Fingertips to ankles
2.0 Survival	201	206	1.2	1.1	34	14	Fingertips 10" below knees
1.5	227	232	1.1	1.0	26	9	Fingertips to knees
1.0 Sickness	245	250	1.0	9	0	0	Fingertips above knees

We may regard the first as personal or intrapersonal motivation and the second as interpersonal relations, which in turn translate to motivation.

Intrapersonal motivation

Intrapersonal motivation is the motivation that occurs within the individual. It incorporates a variety of forces that converge to affect an individual's motivation in life. It deals with the conditions that get people mobilized to invest themselves in efforts. In a very real sense, it describes what makes them tick.

The best way to assess personal motivation is to study an individual's motivation in the various roles in which he or she functions. We can infer from the choices that an individual makes in these roles what the values were that dictated these choices. If we define a career broadly as the way people live their lives (whether in home, school, work, or community associations), we can study a career pattern over time to determine the values that dominate it. Although interviewing and inventorying people, we must exercise care in the respect that stated values are often unrelated to the hard choices an individual must make over a lifetime.

What we can infer is shown in Table 6–3. As can be seen, there are several areas of functioning where we can observe an individual—at home; in continuing education; at work; in the community or the community-at-large, including any local, state, regional,

TABLE 6-3   Levels of intrapersonal motivation

Levels of Functioning	Intrapersonal Motivation			
	Home	*Education*	*Work*	*Community*
5 Missions				
4 Self-fulfillment				
3 Achievement				
2 Incentives				
1 Nonincentive				

national, or international circumstances. Below minimally effective levels (Level 3.0), we can infer choices that were guided by external reinforcement schedules (i.e., outside incentives dictate the person's choices). For example, in our experience, most people choose jobs for such simple reinforcers as money, geography, and sex. Above minimal levels, we can infer choices that were governed by an internalized value system, a sense of self-fulfillment or even a mission outside oneself (Maslow, 1970; McLelland, 1961).

Thus, at the highest level (Level 5.0), people have reasons to live—missions outside of themselves that give meaning to their lives. They are guided by these missions in all aspects of their lives. This motivation may be translated into a personal commitment to abstractions such as social justice. These reasons can be concretized in activities such as serving children or disenfranchised peoples throughout the world or may involve a commitment to an institutionalized mission such as an agency or a community dedicated to the welfare of its members and/or the populations it is servicing. Reduced, this commitment involves nurturing life wherever and whenever it is encountered. Clearly, this level of intrapersonal motivation derives from a commitment beyond one's assigned tasks.

At the next highest level (Level 4.0), people are concerned with fulfilling themselves. Their mission is inside rather than outside themselves. In all situations, they are oriented to learning in order to grow.

At a minimally effective level (Level 3.0), people function to fulfill their need for achievement, including attributes of pride in performance and the work ethic that were instilled in them. They are productive people who follow the initiatives of others, taking great pride in their products, doing what they do very well but seldom doing more than they were asked to do. In this context, they are very attuned to their colleagues and co-workers, are responsive to the latest vogues and "hot-buttons," and are great imitators of the creative thrusts of others.

At the incentive level (Level 2.0), people are controlled by the reinforcement schedules determined by others. They work only to receive rewards such as money, promotions, increased leisure time, country club memberships, and the like. They always do only what is necessary to receive the rewards and are concerned only with marketing themselves to the manipulators of the reinforcement system rather than producing the products for which they are responsible.

At the nonincentive level (Level 1.0), people are not part of the incentive system as we know it. They may have operated within the system and rejected it. Or they may be hooking onto a system to which we are not attuned; for example, the criminal-incentive and career-ladder system that exists in every lower-class community throughout the world. (Crime is a class, not a cultural phenomenon, and the differences between classes are much greater than the differences between cultures.)

One way of checking your own level of intrapersonal motivation is to plot yourself in terms of your daily living. To qualify at any one of these levels of functioning, you must have engaged in at least one act or behavior daily within each of the areas of functioning— home, school, work, community. Thus, to qualify for the incentive level, you must have fulfilled one or more daily objectives that are consistent with being rewarded or avoiding punishment. To qualify at the achievement level, you must have accomplished one or more daily objectives that yield your pride in accomplishment. To qualify at the level of fulfilling yourself, you must have initiated one or more times beyond your daily objectives to find fulfillment in your life. To qualify for actualizing yourself with a mission outside of yourself, you must have completed one or more objectives daily to serve that mission. While the daily requirements are stringent, they emphasize the "way of life" involved in actualizing oneself. If you are not involved in these behaviors on a daily basis, then you are not functioning at any levels of actualization.

Again, for rating this dimension—which we call *emotivation* (the personal motivation dimension of the emotional factors)—we obtain the modal level of functioning or the level at which the person functions most frequently. Included are modal levels both within and between the different areas of functioning, depending upon the purposes of the assessment. These areas include his or her functioning at home, in continuing education, at work, or in the community. In our experience, some people slide up and down this scale, at different points being committed to different motives. Just the fact that a mix of motivations determines different decisions implies a person functioning subliminally at the lowest of these motivation levels. Again, we may most effectively assess the level of motivation by determining an individual's modal level of functioning. It is human to want to use high principled and unselfish motives when the decision does not matter and to get down to the "nitty-gritty" incentives when it does. On the other hand, survival must be assured before growth can take place. In the end, however, those who do not get outside of themselves in their motivation for living do not actualize their human potential.

Interpersonal relations

Interpersonal relations is really a social factor. This factor entails the motivation that derives from becoming involved with someone else. In effect, it involves helping others to develop their motives in life. In so doing, we expand our own boundaries to incorporate their missions as part of our own missions. We see this type of motivation most clearly in terms of helpers' contributions to those most weak and vulnerable members of our society. However, we also see this motivation in the commitments of workers and party members to such causes as nationalism, individual political parties, or corporations.

The best way to assess interpersonal relations is by studying an individual's human relationships in the different areas of his or her life functioning. Thus, we can infer from the individual's overt behavior the level of skills that is offered and the depth of human relations that these skills stimulate. For many people, this determination is quite simple, because they are not even attentive to other people. Therefore, no higher level of human relationship is possible. This level includes most human relationships in our society—relationships that begin at the highest level of attentiveness and gradually fade into oblivion.

What we can observe in interpersonal relations can be seen in Table 6-4. Again, we can make these observations in a variety of areas where the person functions interpersonally—at home, in con-

TABLE 6-4   Levels of interpersonal relations

| | *Interpersonal Relations* | | | |
Areas	*Home*	*Education*	*Work*	*Community*
Levels of Functioning				
5 Initiating				
4 Personalizing				
3 Responding				
2 Attending				
1 Nonattending				

tinuing education, at work, or in the community. Below minimally effective levels (Level 3.0), people are simply attentive in varying degrees to other people. They do not get "inside" others. In some respects, they really do not even stand outside in relation to them. Typically the most difficult skill to teach people in human relations training is to attend to other people. Resistance is encountered in the form of statements such as, "I'm just not comfortable that way." Whether or not being attentive helps them to look and "see" and listen and "hear" others, they really do not want to do it. They are caught up in themselves and unable to relate continuously to others, even physically. Above minimal levels, we observe individuals responding accurately to the people around them (Carkhuff, 1969, 1980).

At the highest level (Level 5.0), initiating, we find individuals not only responding to where people are and personalizing where they want or need to be but also initiating individualized action programs to help them get there. Such individuals help others to achieve their goals.

At level 4.0, personalizing, individuals are responding to facilitate the self-exploration of people and personalizing to facilitate their self-understanding of where they want or need to be. Such individuals help others conceptualize their goals.

At a minimally effective level (Level 3.0), responding, individuals are responding accurately to the feeling and meaning about where people are in their life's experiences as it is expressed by other people. They have, at least, "heard" the other people and communicated their understanding of the others' expressions and, thus, facilitated their exploration.

At level 2.0, attending, we find the individuals being attentive to other people, which means that they are at least involving themselves with others by attending physically, observing, and listening to them.

Level 1.0 is the nonattending level. Here the individuals are inattentive to other people. They do not get involved in any way with others.

One way of checking your own level of interpersonal relations is to plot yourself in terms of your daily living. Again, to qualify at any one of these levels of functioning, you must have engaged in at least one act daily within each area of functioning—home, school, work, community. Thus, to qualify at the attending level, you must have given your full and undivided attention to the appropriate people one or more times on a daily basis. For responding, you must have responded accurately to the expressions of significant others at least once each day. Personalizing requires responding to personalize the goal for each significant person at least once each day. Initiating demands that you initiate to help to develop an action course for each significant person at least once each day. Again, if you do not live it on a daily basis, you do not have it.

The same approach to rating is appropriate: Rate the individual at those levels at which he or she functions most of the time. Thus, the individual is rated at the modal level of functioning either within or between his or her functioning at home, education, work, or in the community. It is noteworthy that individuals who achieve the highest or deepest levels of human relations are always monitoring their levels of understanding by responding interchangeably with other peoples' experience. People who do not have deepening human relations in any arena are never responding accurately to the experiences of others. And all human relations are in the process of deepening or deteriorating! Those whose relationships are deteriorating cannot actualize their human potential. Those whose relationships are deepening can expand their humanity and, ultimately, actualize their human potential.

INTELLECTUAL FACTORS

Intellectual factors attempt to account for the substance, processing, and communication of one's intellectual contribution. There are three dimensions that merge here: The first has to do with the level of development of the person's substantive specialty; the second with the individual's learning skills and processes; the third with the individual's teaching or communication skills.

Substantive specialty

The substantive specialty represents the level of expertise that an individual has achieved in his or her specialty area. It reflects the degree to which he or she has acquired the skills and knowledge necessary to discharge responsibilities. One's substantive specialty may be a vocational responsibility or it may be an avocational interest. Reduced, substantive specialty is what a person's life is about. Substantive specialty encompasses the content that he or she has mastered and applied in a continuing cycle of learning. The test is whether an individual has the skills and knowledge sufficient to achieve the goals of oneself and others in the area. In other words, the test is whether a person can be creative and productive in his or her area of substance.

The support factors in this test involve whether one has the knowledge necessary to be creative and productive. The heart of the test of creativity is whether an individual can operationalize any goal in his or her substantive specialty. The heart of the test of productivity is whether one can develop the systems and technology to achieve any goal. What makes a person truly a professional in any area of endeavor is the ability to operationalize and technologize the achievement of a goal. Few people ever achieve this status because they will not pay the price of hard work and discipline necessary to be true professionals: They operate only in the realm of facts and concepts, the language of which many become quick studies in acquiring.

As can be seen in Table 6-5, below minimally effective levels (Level 3.0), people have only the factual and conceptual knowledge about any phenomena in their specialty areas. In reality, they have only an idea of what is to happen in any given circumstance. Typically, this vague comprehension is enough to get them by in most areas—to say the "right" words and behave the "right" way is sufficient to confuse others who are themselves only imitating some localized language and behavior. Above minimal levels, people incorporate knowledge as supportive of the skills they employ in designing and implementing the achievement of their goal (Berenson, Berenson, and Carkhuff, 1977; Carkhuff, 1980). Again, these

TABLE 6-5   Levels of substantive specialty

Areas	Substantive Specialty			
	Home	Education	Work	Community

Levels of
Functioning

5 Technology development

4 Goal operationalization

3 Principles application

2 Conceptual knowledge

1 Factual knowledge

applications can occur in a variety of areas of functioning, including home, education, work, and the community.

At the highest level (Level 5.0), technology development, people develop and implement the technologies and systems needed to achieve their goals. This level represents an operational definition of productivity and usually requires permutations and combinations of all of the skills and skill steps available to an individual in his or her arsenal of responses in the substantive specialty.

At the next highest level (Level 4.0), goal operationalization, people are capable of operationalizing any goals; that is, developing the operations needed to achieve the goals. These operations include the design of the systems and technologies required to answer the fundamental questions of goal operationalization: (1) Who is doing what (to whom); (2) at what level; and (3) under what conditions, including where and when. The design of the systems needed to answer these questions is, itself, an operational definition of goal operationalization.

At a minimally effective level (Level 3.0), the application of principles, we find people answering the question, "Why?" Individuals functioning at this level know why a given phenomenon does what it does. Although they have not yet made the applications, they know how the different components and processes interact and how to translate these principles to applications.

At a less-than-minimally effective level (Level 2.0), conceptual knowledge, persons have only an awareness of the concepts of a given phenomenon. That is to say, they can only conceptualize what it does and not why and how.

Level 1.0 involves factual knowledge. Here people have an awareness only of what the phenomenon is and not what it does or why and how it does it. Both of the latter two less-than-minimally facilitative levels place a lid on an individual's ability to apply what he or she has learned, and yet they are the levels that are emphasized in most educational programs.

To check your own level of development in your substantive specialty, you may plot your daily functioning in your different areas of application—home, school, work, community. To qualify at the factual level, you must have engaged each day in gathering one or more of the facts you need to discharge your specialty responsibilities in at least one of the application areas. For the conceptual level, you must have engaged each day in developing one or more of the concepts involved in your specialty. For the principle level, you must have interrelated the facts and concepts and developed at least one new principle in your specialty each day. At the goal operationalization level, you must operationalize at least one new goal in your specialty each day. Finally, at the technology development level, you must outline at least one program to achieve your operational goal each day. While the requirements for rating are stringent, they reflect the level of your involvement in self-actualization activities.

Again, we rate individuals according to their modal levels of functioning. Thus, the individual is rated at the level that dominates either within or between his or her functioning at home, in continuing education, at work, or in the community. It is noteworthy that individuals functioning modally above minimally effective levels are always operationalizing and technologizing applications in their substantive specialty and learning from these applications. People functioning below minimally effective levels are never making applications simply because they do not know why or how to do so. And if we cannot operationalize and technologize goals, we cannot achieve them. Thus, we cannot be actualized in our substantive specialty area. We cannot actualize if we do not operationalize.

Learning skills

Learning skills represent the level of expertise an individual has achieved in generic learning ability. That is to say, generic learning ability is the capacity to approach any learning situation—new or old—with an effective system for processing. To do so requires an involvement in the learning process through an open reception to the input data. It involves the effective processing of the data by breaking it down into its components, processes, and functions and analyzing one's relationship to that data. It means funneling that data toward a goal and focusing one's efforts upon output. In short, learning skills represent the process by which the individual transforms selected input into focused output.

The test of learning skills is whether an individual can discern where he or she is in relation to a given phenomenon; can determine where he or she is in relation to where he or she wants or needs to be with that phenomenon; and can develop a means to get there. Involved is a kind of self-diagnosis that we may call exploration; a goal-setting that we may call understanding; and an initiative program that we may call action. While many people involve themselves in learning to the degree that they receive the input, few ever explore themselves effectively; fewer still understand their relationships to a goal; and the fewest act to achieve the goal. Less than one person in one hundred has developed an effective learning system that recycles the feedback from acting to stimulate more extensive exploration, more accurate understanding, more effective action.

As can be seen in Table 6–6, below minimally effective levels (Level 3.0), people become involved at most in receiving the input concerning any phenomena. At this stage they are at their all-time best. Indeed, they have cultivated all of their characteristics to look attentive, appear concerned, and ask apparently astute questions. I am reminded of the thousands of tapes I have heard and seen of initial interactions in helping and teaching. The image that comes to mind is one of the social worker conducting an intake interview: After hearing a despairing story of overwhelming crisis, he or she asks: "How old did you say you were?" A main factor emerging from any analysis of intake interviews is the "stupid question factor." On the other hand, above minimal levels, people explore, understand, and act effectively upon the different areas of their environments (Carkhuff and Berenson, 1976, 1982).

At the highest level (Level 5.0), action skills, people develop action programs to get from where they are to where they want or need to be. Obviously, action is a cumulative skill that incorporates exploring where individuals are and understanding where they want or need to be.

At the next highest level (Level 4.0), understanding skills, people develop an understanding of where they are going, of where they want or need to be in relation to the particular learning experience

TABLE 6-6 Levels of learning skills

	Learning Skills Areas			
Areas	Home	Education	Work	Community

Levels of
Functioning

5 Acting

4 Understanding

3 Exploring

2 Involving

1 Noninvolving

involved. Clearly, an accurate grasp of one's goals implies an extensive exploration of one's circumstance.

At a minimally effective level (Level 3.0), exploring skills, people explore where they are in relation to the learning experience. In effect they analyze the components, processes, and functions of the experience and of themselves in relation to the experience to determine where they are.

At a less-than-minimally effective level (Level 2.0), people engage only in the apparently attentive behaviors that receive the input data concerning the learning experience. They do not go on to process the data.

Finally, at the lowest level (Level 1.0), people do not become involved in learning. They do not receive input, let alone process it.

To check out your own level of learning activities, you may plot your daily functioning in your different areas of application—home, school, work, community. To qualify, you must have engaged in at least one learning activity in your substantive specialty in at least one application area each day—becoming involved in one or more learning activities for the involvement levels; exploring where you are one or more times for the exploration level; understanding where you want to be for the understanding level; acting to get to your goals for the action level. Again, the stringent learning requirements reflect learning as a way of life.

Here too we rate individuals modally, both within and between their areas of functioning—at home, in continuing education, at work, or in the community. It is to be emphasized that people functioning modally above minimally effective levels are always processing data; that is, they are always learning. People functioning below minimally effective levels are never processing data and thus are never learning. We are fully alive only if we are fully learning. We can only actualize our human potential with an effective learning system.

Teaching skills

Teaching skills represent the level of expertise that an individual has in teaching his or her substantive learnings. Teaching involves the ability to communicate skills and knowledge. The process involved is the other side of learning. Whereas learning involves one's own development of a course of action based upon understanding or insight, teaching involves helping others to develop courses of action based upon their understanding or insights. In short, teaching facilitates someone else's learning.

The test of teaching, then, is whether one person can help others to explore where they are in relation to a given phenomenon; help them to understand where they want or need to be; and help them to develop action programs to get there. That individual is diagnosing, setting goals, and individualizing learning programs with and for others. These skills facilitate the exploration, understanding, and action learning process of others. While many people develop at least the conceptual content of their substantive specialty, few ever reach the stage of being able to diagnose accurately someone else's functioning in terms of that content; setting goals in terms of the results of the diagnosis; and individualizing learning programs in terms of the goals.

As can be seen in Table 6-7, below minimally effective levels (Level 3.0), people develop their content, at most. At that, they tend to develop it only at a conceptual level. In other words, they know what it is they want to teach, but they do not communicate it. We all remember the dominant experiences of our education: The teacher lectures didactically about factual and conceptual knowledge. There is no effort made to meet the conditions of learning by facilitating the learning process of exploration, understanding, and action. Consequently, beyond third grade (until which teachers actually engage in teaching) learning is decremental. Above minimally effective levels, people not only know their content but have developed the means of communicating it to other people in the different areas of their environment—at home, in continuing education, at work,

TABLE 6-7   Levels of teaching skills

		Teaching Skills			
Areas	*Home*	*Education*	*Work*	*Community*

Levels of Functioning

5   Individualizing programs

4   Goal-setting

3   Diagnosing

2   Developing content

1   No content

and in the community (Berenson, Berenson, and Carkhuff, 1978a, 1978b, 1979; Carkhuff, 1981; Carkhuff and Berenson, 1976).

At the highest level (Level 5.0), individualizing programs, people develop and individualize learning programs for others. These individualized learning programs facilitate the action learning of others. They insure that others receive and learn the substance that they are delivering. Obviously, individualizing programs incorporate goal-setting and diagnosis in terms of the content being communicated.

At the next level (Level 4.0), goal-setting, people develop goals for and with other people. Goal-setting skills enable the other people to understand where they are going. These skills, in turn, incorporate diagnostic and content development skills.

At a minimally effective level (Level 3.0), diagnosing, people can diagnose others in terms of their levels of functioning on the content involved. This diagnosis facilitates the learners' exploration of where they are in relation to the content and implies the development of the content.

At a less-than-minimally effective level (Level 2.0), the people only develop their content at the level that they have conquered their substantive specialty. In other words, even if they have the content to teach, they do not know how to communicate it.

Finally, at the lowest level (Level 1.0), people do not even develop their content in a manner that others could receive it. They do not develop their own contributions, let alone attempt to communicate them.

To check out your own level of teaching activities, you may plot your daily functioning in your different areas of application—home, school, work, community. To qualify for any level of functioning, you must have engaged in at least one teaching activity to deliver your substantive specialty in at least one application area each day. Thus, for the content development level, you must have developed some content each day; for the diagnostic level, you must have diagnosed at least one learner's level of functioning in your specialty area each day; for the goal-setting level, you must have set at least one learner's goal in your specialty area each day; for the individualizing level, you must have developed at least one individualized program for at least one learner in your specialty area each day. The stringent teaching requirements reflect the necessity for communication as part of your intellectual development.

Again, we rate the individuals modally, both within and between their areas of functioning. It is noteworthy that people above minimally effective levels are always communicating their content effectively: They are accurately sensing where others are; effectively determining goals for where they want or need to be; and initiatively developing individualized action programs to get them there. They are always teaching. People functioning below minimally effective levels are never communicating their ideas and skills. They are never teaching. Teachers are learners because of the feedback they receive from teaching. Thus, only people who teach what it is they are about can actualize their potential in what it is they are about. Only teachers can be actualizers.

In summary, each rating scale can be used to measure an individual's performance on the dimension involved. In addition, each dimension can be seen in relation to the other dimensions. Thus, the physical dimensions serve to provide the energy for the other functions. The intrapersonal motivation dimension serves as a catalyst to the other dimensions. The interpersonal relations dimension functions to expand the base of motivation to incorporate the frames of reference of other people. The substantive specialty represents the individual's intellectual creativity and productivity. The learning skills operate to guide the individual's processing of all input and focusing of all output. And the teaching skills function to communicate the substantive learnings and, in interaction with the recipients, to generate the individual's involvement in a life-long learning process.

Again, the stringent requirements reflect the demands of functioning effectively at any level. At the highest levels, they reflect the rigorous demands that define a fully functioning person. Indeed, they define such a person as a human being. The fact that very few people function effectively at even the most minimal levels of functioning is testimony to the fact that many people function at less than human levels.

In the end, the power of actualizing human potential lies in the actualizing of the intellectual factors that the physical factors serve to energize and the emotional factors serve to catalyze. The heart of the contribution of the intellectual factors lies in the ability to learn and teach how to operationalize and technologize goals in a substantive area. Those who can help human beings to achieve human goals can help themselves to achieve their human potential.

REFERENCES

Berenson, D. H.; Berenson, S. R., and Carkhuff, R. R. *The Skills of Teaching—Content Development Skills*. Amherst, Mass.: Human Resource Development Press, 1978.

————. *The Skills of Teaching—Lesson Planning Skills.* Amherst, Mass.: Human Resource Development Press, 1978.

Berenson, S. R.; Berenson, D. H.; and Carkhuff, R. R. *The Skills of Teaching—Teaching Delivery Skills.* Amherst, Mass.: Human Resource Development Press, 1979.

Carkhuff, R. R. *The Art of Program Development.* Amherst, Mass.: Human Resource Development Press, 1974.

————. *The Art of Helping IV.* Amherst, Mass.: Human Resource Development Press, 1980.

————. *The Skilled Teacher.* Amherst, Mass.: Human Resource Development Press, in press, 1981.

Carkhuff, R. R. and Berenson, B. G. *Teaching as Treatment.* Amherst, Mass.: Human Resource Development Press, 1976.

Carkhuff, R. R. and Berenson, D. H. *Learning to Learn.* Amherst, Mass.: Carkhuff Institute of Human Technology, in press, 1981.

Carkhuff, R. R.; Berenson, D. H.; and Pierce, R. M. *The Skills of Teaching—Interpersonal Skills.* Amherst, Mass.: Human Resource Development Press, 1977.

Collingwood, T. R. The Carkhuff Human Resource Development Model and Physical Fitness. In D. W. Kratochvil (Ed.) *Carkhuff: The HRD Model in Education.* Baton Rouge: Southern University, 1973.

Collingwood, T. R. and Carkhuff, R. R. *Get Fit for Living.* Amherst, Mass.: Human Resource Development Press, 1974.

Maslow, A. H. *Motivation and Personality.* New York: Harper and Row, 1970.

McLelland, D. *The Achieving Society.* New York: Van Nostrand Reinhold, 1961.

7
The data of actualizing

A long time ago back in the 1960s, when I, along with a number of graduate students, was diligently engaged in human relations research, I came upon a simple but astonishing finding: By far the great majority of people were functioning at extraordinarily low levels of human relations. In research terms, selecting people at random did not give us enough variability to measure anything. While people might specialize in certain behaviors like "looking interested" or "asking questions," it did not matter functionally. At most, they were attentive. At least, they were oblivious to other human beings. In either event, they were not involved beyond attentiveness with another human being. To be sure, in one instance, one student brought back data that prompted me to challenge the randomness of his selection because the subjects he researched were the lowest functioning humanoid-types that I had ever heard. We found out later that these subjects were the campus leaders, the speech-makers, the "communicators," the future politicians of America.

In any case, we resolved this research problem by selecting people who were functioning at high levels in human relations and comparing their outcomes with those of people who were matched and/or randomly selected as functioning at moderate or low levels. On every index assessed, the results were dramtically different in favor of the high-functioning people.

Our research problem in assessing human potential is similar: We needed to find people who were highly creative and productive and compare their levels of functioning on human potential dimensions with people who were not highly creative and productive. We did this by first assessing the excellence of the products and then measuring the levels of functioning of producers and nonproducers.

THE RESEARCH PROCESS

It is, to be sure, difficult to postulate and measure the dimensions of human potential. I will describe the course we followed over the span of two decades of research and application (see Figure 7–1). With our interest in developing human resources, we observed extensive bodies of stable phenomena. In making these observations, we incorporated learnings from a variety of different orientations, especially the client-centered, trait-and-factor, and behavioristic approaches. What we learned is that certain people were more effective in accomplishing their purposes in parenting, helping, teaching, and managing. We induced some generalizations from their behaviors, postulating and operationalizing their behaviors on a

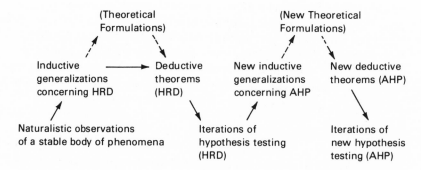

Figure 7-1 The inductive and deductive processes in operationalizing the dimensions of human potential

variety of measurable indices of such dimensions as interpersonal skills, teaching skills, learning skills, or management skills. We deduced some theorems from these generalizations and formulated them in testable hypotheses.

What we found was that people functioning at high levels of human dimensions such as interpersonal skills or teaching skills or learning skills were eminently more successful in accomplishing their objectives than were people functioning at low levels of these skills. Thus, we found them to be more effective in helping people, teaching people, and learning things as measured by a variety of indices (Anthony, 1978; Aspy and Roebuck, 1978; Carkhuff, 1969, 1971; Rogers, Gendlin, Kiesler, and Truax, 1967; Truax and Carkhuff, 1967). This, in turn, led us to the development of an extensive number of training programs in living, learning, and working skills—skills that enable people to live, learn, and work more effectively. We studied the effects of these programs in a number of iterations of hypothesis testing and found the applications of the skills learned to be effective in many important ways (Carkhuff and Berenson, 1976).

We collected a great deal of data and made a huge number of observations of people functioning in many roles—as spouses and parents, as teachers and counselors, as administrators and supervisors. We began to make inductive generalizations from a stable body of phenomena produced by our hypothesis testing: People who were rated high on certain of these dimensions were effective in accomplishing their goals; more important for our purposes, they seemed to be people who were beginning to approximate fulfilling their potential. For example, as we indicated in Chapter 4, such people had physical fitness programs, were very highly motivated, applied their interpersonal skills with great sensitivity, developed a high level of expertise in their substantive specialty, had open and responsive learning systems, were effective teachers and communicators. Above all, they worked very hard and were very disciplined at everything they were doing. Ironically, it was this discipline in acquiring and applying their responses that was the source of their great spontaneity and creativity: The greater the quantity of responses was, the higher the quality of creativity.

At the same time, we attempted to incorporate the learnings from other people concerned with actualizing human potential. The only significant piece of input came from the one serious scholar in pursuit of actualizing human potential, Abraham Maslow (1972). While some of his emphases upon cultural and philosophical dimensions were not incorporated except in the assumptions that self-actualizing people made about their lives, much of it provided a great richness in elaborating upon the emotional and interpersonal dimensions—and to a lesser degree upon the intellectual dimensions. Thus, armed with our own research and observations and enriched by the learnings from the work of Maslow and his associates, we proceeded through iterations of definitions and testing to measure the dimensions of human potential.

THE RESEARCH CONTEXT

A combination of observations and inventories and interviews were employed over a period of two years to distinguish the differences between actualizers and non-actualizers. Actualizers were identified as persons who produced products rated by a panel of experts as excellent or superior in one or more areas of functioning. Non-actualizers were drawn from pools of people who, in spite of having similar backgrounds and exposures, did not produce any highly rated products. We do not acknowledge that it is possible to actualize one's potential without having impact upon the environment, including people, in which one lives. And the most direct way of evaluating this impact is to assess some product.

Twenty actualizers and eighty non-actualizers were identified according to their productivity. The process of identifying the actualizers took place over a period of ten years' study. Non-actualizers were people drawn from similar working environments with similar backgrounds and exposures. The actualizers all produced at least one product—books or articles or copyrighted materials, patented inventions or methodologies, recognized administrative procedures, or the like—in one of the physical, emotional, intellectual, or career areas. In one instance, one person produced high rated products in all of the areas indicated. The non-actualizers produced no products rated at levels of excellence by the panel of experts.

It is to be emphasized that the numbers do not represent a random sampling. The actualizers were identified over a period of years and the non-actualizers were selected to match them in experiences. Both were then observed and inventoried and interviewed under circumstances of random sampling.

Of the twenty actualizers, five were women and two were minorities. Eleven were in their late thirties, six were in their forties, and three were in their fifties. The non-actualizers followed approximately the same distribution with the dominant ages in the thirties, forties, and fifties.

The ratings were based upon a combination of inventories and observations and were made by two trained raters who, themselves, would qualify as actualizers by any criteria. The inter-rater reliabilities of the expert raters ranged in the high .90s for all dimensions.

As can be seen, Table 7–1 summarizes the six dimensions under the physical, emotional, and intellectual areas of functioning. Also, for summary purposes the levels of functioning between dimensions are collapsed and new categories introduced. The Actualizer level includes those persons who, by their modal levels of functioning, demonstrate that they are moving toward actualization of their human potential. They function physically with stamina; emotionally with a mission and interpersonally with initiative; intellectually with technological proficiency, action learning, and individualized teaching programs. They are initiative Actualizers in life.

Similarly, at the Contributor level, people function physically with intensity in selective areas; emotionally with a personal goal of fulfilling themselves and an interpersonal goal of helping others to personalize their goals; intellectually with the ability to operationalize goals in their substantive specialty, to understand their own goals, and to help others to understand theirs. They are creative Contributors to life.

At the Participant level, people function physically with adaptability to the tasks at hand; emotionally with a need to achieve and interpersonally with an ability to respond to others; intellectually with the principles of their specialty, learning skills for exploring where they are, and diagnostic skills for helping others to explore where they are. They are active Participants in life.

At the Observer level, the people function physically at the survival level; emotionally on the incentive schedule and interpersonally at the level of attentiveness to others; intellectually at the level of concepts, with minimum involvement in learning and with only their content, conceptual as it is, in teaching.

Finally, at the Detractor level, the people are not able to survive physically; they are not involved motivationally or interpersonally; they have only factual knowledge of their substantive areas and no learning or teaching skills intellectually.

Of course, not all individuals fall neatly into one or another level of profile. However, in general, past research has taught us that the higher an individual is functioning on one index, the higher he or she tends to function on other indices. In other words, at higher levels of functioning, there tends to be a consistency across dimensions. At lower levels, while people may specialize in any one area of

TABLE 7-1 Areas and levels of functioning

DIMENSIONS OF HUMAN POTENTIAL

Levels of functioning	Physical	Emotional			Intellectual	
	(Fitness)	(Motivation)	(Interpersonal)	(Substance)	(Learning)	(Teaching)
5 ACTUALIZERS	Stamina	Mission	Initiating	Technologizing	Acting	Individualizing
4 CONTRIBUTORS	Intensity	Self-fulfill	Personalizing	Operational-izing	Understanding	Goal-setting
3 PARTICIPANTS	Adaptability	Achievement	Responding	Principles	Exploring	Diagnosing
2 OBSERVERS	Nonadapt	Incentive	Attending	Concepts	Involvement	Content development
1 DETRACTORS	Sick	Nonincentive	Nonattentive	Facts	Noninvolve-ment	Unprepared

functioning, there is no discernible pattern. For example, there is no relationship between dimensions such as discrimination and communication in a given area. In addition, even on their relatively highest indices, individuals functioning at relatively low levels (such as the Observer level) never approach the relatively lowest indices of high-level functioning people (such as the Contributor level).

THE DATA

As can be seen in Figure 7–2, there are significant differences in functioning between actualizers and non-actualizers. Actualizers average a modal level of functioning above Level 4.0, while non-actualizers approximate a modal level of functioning of Level 2.0. What this means functionally is that actualizers are in control of their lives and able to contribute to their worlds. In turn, non-actualizers are caught up within themselves, manipulated by their worlds, and unable to participate fully in them.

Within the actualizers' profiles, it can be seen that they tend to emphasize intellectual excellence. Although their fitness levels are more than adequate to allow them to engage in their pursuits with intensity; their emotivation level suggests a concern primarily with personal fulfillment; and their interpersonal relations are conducted at a highly personalized level, the subjects seem to most closely approximate actualizing themselves in the intellectual area. Here actualizers tend toward developing their substantive products fully to the most atomistic level of implementation. Similarly, in learning

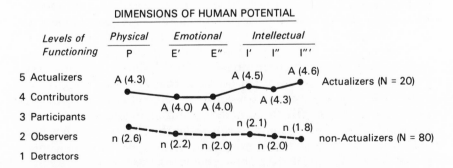

Figure 7-2   Profiles of Actualizers and Non-actualizers

programs they tend toward detailed planning and action programs. Finally, they appear to be functioning at the highest levels of teaching and communicating their substantive knowledge through individualizing the learning programs of their recipients. Clearly, for actualizers, the physical and emotional dimensions seem to serve supportive roles to making intellectual thrusts. And in those thrusts they are characterized by their detailed activities of planning, implementation, evaluation, and recycling for new learnings.

Within the non-actualizers' profiles, the results are quite different. Here, the subjects are functioning at the highest levels physically—approaching a level of adaptability. It is noteworthy that the physical area is the easiest in which to improve and maintain some minimal level of functionality. Further, personal motivation lands squarely within reach of the incentive systems; interpersonal relationships are, at best, attentive; the substantive pursuits are limited to the conceptual and the linguistic levels; learning is never more than a highly tentative involvement; and teaching is a neglected and unknown quantity, even for "professional" teachers. Clearly, non-actualizers rate higher physically than they do in any other area. And this, if anything, typifies their behavior—being at their best at first appearance and at their worst in delivery and follow-through.

The trait that most distinguishes actualizers from non-actualizers is the systematic nature of their programs. Actualizers have systematic programs for maintenance and improvement in all areas. Non-actualizers do not. The actualizers all have regular physical fitness programs; they all have programs for working upon objectives that fulfill themselves and their missions on a daily basis; they all have programs for responding interpersonally to their loved ones, friends, students or teachers, and employees or employers; they all have programs for achieving objectives in their substantive specialty on a daily basis; they all have learning programs for improving their knowledge and skills in their specialty area; they all have teaching programs for communicating their learnings.

On the other hand, when they have programs, the non-actualizers usually do so only in the physical area. Even at that, these programs are often contaminated by concerns for losing weight and making a nice appearance. In contrast, the actualizers' concerns are for being physically fit and having sufficient energy to manage the often enormous and complex schedules they have. Some few non-actualizers have systematic programs in the emotional and intellectual areas, but most often these programs appear to be prompted by external circumstances such as a class they are taking or a crisis they are experiencing. For example, one such person got involved in working regularly on a book for parents of children with congenital heart disease after the death of an infant daughter while another started to programmatically use the interpersonal skills she was learning in a class. Mostly, the non-actualizers see their emotional and intellectual programs in conventional ways such as reading and studying and working for degrees. In contrast, the actualizers see their programs in terms of their functional utility in fulfilling themselves and their missions in life.

In summary, actualizers are characterized by high levels of resource development and the excellence of their product contribution as they strive toward self-actualization. They are integrated internally and committed to fulfilling themselves and mastering their fates. Non-actualizers, in contrast, may be described in terms of their low levels of resource development and the absence of values products as they observe themselves and their worlds being manipulated. It is as if they are outside of themselves—viewing themselves as objects rather than controlling their own destinies.

The measurement of human potential has direct implications for actualizing human potential. Clearly, being able to diagnose oneself in any one or all areas of functioning directly affects setting goals in any one or all areas. Thus, if an individual is diagnosed at the adaptive level physically, he or she may set goals for achieving the intensity level of functioning. Similarly, if an individual is functioning modally as a Participant, he or she may set goals for functioning as a Contributor. Each level of rating becomes a sub-goal in an overall program for actualizing human potential. Detailed individualized programs can be developed to reach each of these sub-goals.

In this context, there are a number of existing teaching or training programs for increasing functioning in the human potential dimensions: physical fitness (Carkhuff, 1974; Collingwood and Carkhuff, 1975); intrapersonal motivation (Maslow, 1970; McLelland, 1961); interpersonal relations (Carkhuff, 1969, 1980); substantive specialty (Berenson, Berenson, and Carkhuff, 1978a; Carkhuff and Berenson, 1976); learning skills (Carkhuff and Berenson, 1976, 1981); teaching skills (Carkhuff, 1981; Carkhuff, Berenson, and Pierce, 1977; Berenson, Berenson, and Carkhuff, 1978a, 1978b, 1979). Thus, individuals can develop their own self-actualization program by learning the generic skills and knowledge involved in the development of each dimension. Again and most important, they can actualize their human potential by hard and disciplined work over a lifetime.

In conclusion, the actualizer is a learner, a person who has freed himself or herself from the conditioning schedule. Learning, unlike conditioning, is not limited by the original stimulus complex; learning always involves entering the learner's frame of reference to determine response needs and always includes transferable strategies. Learning requires operationalized goals and programmatic steps to achieve the goal whereas conditioning is dependent upon externally determined objectives. Learning involves the production of behavior based upon input whereas conditioning involves the reproduction of behavior whenever the learner is presented with the original stimulus complex. In this context, once the learner has conquered the conditioning schedule, the schedule itself becomes one more of the many responses in his or her response repertoire to be used as appropriate to achieve useful goals. In the end, the functional intelligence of the actualizer is a function of the number of systems he or she has conquered as a learner. When the learner conquers a system, then the learner can learn something new—thus, the elevating, spiraling cycle of learning and growth of responses.

The main value of this research is its potentially great heuristic value in understanding and operationalizing the dimensions of actualizing human potential. In addition, it has stimulated many serendipitous learnings—some remaining yet to be operationalized. If we allow human potential to remain only in the realm of human experience—and not to become measurable—then we, ourselves, have not fulfilled our potential through the use of our experience and our intellect.

Again, the words of one of our actualizers echo words said long ago: "To him who knoweth to do truth and doeth it not, to him it is sin."

REFERENCES

Anthony, W.C. *The Principles of Psychiatric Rehabilitation*. Amherst, Mass.: Human Resource Development Press, 1978.

Aspy, D. N. and Roebuck, F. N. *KIDS Don't Learn from People They Don't Like*. Amherst, Mass.: Human Resource Development Press, 1977.

Berenson, D. H.; Berenson, S. R.; and Carkhuff, R. R. *The Skills of Teaching—Content Development Skills*. Amherst, Mass.: Human Resource Development Press, 1978.

——— . *The Skills of Teaching—Lesson Planning Skills*. Amherst, Mass.: Human Resource Development Press, 1978.

Berenson, S. B.; Berenson, D. H.; and Carkhuff, R. R. *The Skills of Teaching—Teaching Delivery Skills*. Amherst, Mass.: Human Resource Development Press, 1979.

Carkhuff, R. R. *Helping and Human Relations, Vols. I and II*. New York: Holt, Rinehart and Winston, 1969.

————. *The Development of Human Resources*. New York: Holt, Rinehart and Winston, 1971.

————. *The Art of Program Development*. Amherst, Mass.: Human Resource Development Press, 1974.

————. *The Art of Helping IV*. Amherst, Mass.: Human Resource Development Press, 1980.

————. *The Art and Science of Teaching*. Amherst, Mass.: Human Resource Development Press, in press, 1981.

Carkhuff, R. R. and Berenson, B. G. *Teaching as Treatment*. Amherst, Mass.: Human Resource Development Press, 1976.

Carkhuff, R. R. and Berenson, D. H. *Learning to Learn*. Amherst, Mass.: Carkhuff Institute of Human Technology, in press, 1981.

Carkhuff, R. R.; Berenson, D. H.; and Pierce, R. M. *The Skills of Teaching—Interpersonal Skills*. Amherst, Mass.: Human Resource Development Press, 1977.

Collingwood, T. R. The Carkhuff Human Resource Development Model and Physical Fitness. In D. W. Kratochvil (Ed.) *Carkhuff: The HRD Model in Education*. Baton Rouge: Southern University Press, 1973.

Collingwood, T. and Carkhuff, R. R. *Get Fit for Living*. Amherst, Mass.: Human Resource Development Press, 1974.

Maslow, A. H. *Motivation and Personality*. New York: Harper and Row, 1970.

McLelland, D. *The Achieving Society*. New York: Van Nostrand Reinhold, 1961.

Rogers, C. R.; Gendlin, E.; Kiesler, D.; and Truax, C. B. *The Therapeutic Relationship and Its Impact*. Madison, Wisconsin: University of Wisconsin Press, 1967.

Truax, C. B. and Carkhuff, R. R. *Toward Effective Counseling and Psychotherapy*. Chicago: Aldine, 1967.

8
Some case studies in actualizing

We all know in our guts the feeling of being in the presence of fully functioning people. Perhaps we were truly fortunate and had one or more as parents. Or maybe we benefited from having a few as teachers. Or maybe we encountered a few in other roles in our lives. What they all have in common is a sense of contrast with other people: They are simply not like others. We hear many things about them:

> *"They are egotistical." (translation:* fit)
> *"They march to the tune of a different drummer." (translation:* independent)
> *"They are soft." (translation:* sensitive)
> *"They are arrogant." (translation:* truthful)
> *"They are naive." (translation:* learners)
> *"They are rigid." (translation:* programmatic)

In sum, they are like alien creatures from another time and place who walk among us. Alien not because they are less

*human—but because they are more human. Because they have
chosen to become who they can be. Because they have decided,
whatever the price, to use their seventy-odd years here on earth
to fulfill themselves—and to help others do the same. Because
they are committed to actualizing their human potential. Alien in
relation to us, Yes! Alienated from humanity, No! Never! They
are the only humanity this planet has ever known.*

The differences between actualizers and non-actualizers are not only
quantitative. The differences are qualitative. Aside from the different assumptions they make about themselves and their worlds,
the differences above and below minimally effective levels of functioning are dramatic.

Below minimally effective levels of physical functioning, non-
actualizers are struggling simply to maintain themselves and adapt
to the circumstances of their daily living. Above minimally effective
levels of functioning, actualizers are developing fitness programs to
increase their energy supply so that they can focus with intensity
and stamina upon the efforts implementing their missions in life.
They are continually expanding their energy supplies so that they
can be on the initiative rather than the defensive in life.

Below minimal levels of emotivational functioning, non-
actualizers are victims of their reinforcement schedules. Above minimally effective levels, actualizers are not only free of external reinforcements but are committed to internalized missions that manipulate externalized reinforcement systems: Having freed themselves
of the reinforcement systems, they manipulate them to help to free
other people.

Below minimal levels interpersonally, non-actualizers are unable to relate to other humans—to touch soul-to-soul without their
bodies touching. Above minimal levels, actualizers not only relate
to other humans but incorporate their humanity in their own: They
are continually expanding the boundaries of their own humanity,
and with that, the missions of their existence.

Below minimal levels substantively, non-actualizers are not on
top of their subject matter; at best, they are struggling to understand
the principles involved. Above minimal levels, actualizers are on top
of their subject matter. They can create and operationalize new goals
and develop programs to achieve them.

Below minimal levels of learning, non-actualizers hardly
enter the learning process. When they do, it never goes beyond the
exploring phase at one extreme. Or, at the other extreme, they enter

directly into the action phase without the benefit of exploration and understanding. Above minimal levels, actualizers cannot only understand their goals and act to achieve them but also recycle them in a life-long learning process.

Below minimal levels of teaching, non-actualizers usually do no more than develop their content and sometimes diagnose the recipients in terms of the content: They do not know how to communicate their content and enable a recipient to function productively with it. Above minimal levels, actualizers can set differential teaching goals based on differential diagnoses and develop individualized learning programs to achieve those teaching goals.

In summary, non-actualizers are victims of their worlds, entrapped by its systems and struggling only to survive. Actualizers are creators of their worlds, conquerors of its systems, and committed only to growing. The former are dying and deathly in all of their relations. The latter are alive and vital in all of their relations.

In my study of actualizers, I found they were all in command of themselves and their worlds yet committed to constructive purposes for both. In addition, whatever the reason—whether by choice or birth—all were on the margin of society, pursuing their causes and fulfilling their contributions.

The following are case studies of actualizers, each of whom I have had the opportunity to observe and interview as well as to review their products over a period of at least ten years. I present them, with permission, not so much as biographical case studies but as illustrations of the approach to operationalizing and measuring the dimensions of the actualization of human potential.

ACTUALIZERS: CASE STUDIES

I offer three people for study and analysis. Two are in their midforties and one is in his early fifties. The criteria that distinguish them as actualizers are at least threefold: (1) the creative products they have produced in pursuit of their personal missions; (2) the creative processes in which they have engaged to produce their products; (3) the fact that they have persevered over their lifetimes—in the face of all obstacles and crises—to pursue their missions. They come from different walks of life—business, government, education, association, and community work—and at different points have engaged in different careers. They differ in many respects except for the fact that, wherever they started, these particular subjects have ultimately converged upon education as the vehicle to serve their respective missions in the same way that it provided them with an opportunity to fulfill themselves (although this is not a necessary characteristic of actualizers).

Shirley McCune

Shirley McCune grew up on a ranch in Colorado, the oldest of three children. Her parents were ranchers and until Shirley reached adolescence, she tended cattle and mended fence with the best of them. Indeed, it was the experience of reaching puberty and being excluded from many more masculine experiences that helped to shape Shirley's current mission of achieving equity for women. She was deeply hurt at the time, because she did not understand why she was deprived of the experiences which the boys had. She understands it now as a deficit in the response repertoires of the people around her which in turn caused a response deficit in women: They do not learn to cooperate as a team to achieving a goal; while they learn to respond to the needs of others, they do not learn to initiate on their own behalf. Accordingly, Shirley has spent her mature professional years in pursuit of equity or in her words "... not just the equality but the quality of experience for women." At present, Shirley is discharging her commitment in her position as Deputy Assistant Secretary of Education in charge of Equal Educational Opportunity Programs, Department of Education.

From the beginning, Shirley sees the significant source of effect upon her maturity as having been growing up in a rural environment. There she learned the "values organized around independence, productivity, and the fundamental worth of all human beings." At the same time, she had the special privilege of being exposed to a variety of unusual mentors, including especially her father. These mentors have served as role models for her in later life, particularly in a work environment.

From the beginning, Shirley has distinguished herself by her ability to achieve, initially in areas of educational and musical excellence. Over the last decade, she has transferred this achievement ethic into the realm of human rights, especially feminine equity. As Director of the Resource Center for Sex and Race Equity of the Council of Chief State School Officers, Shirley and her associates developed the measures to close the gap for full equity for all children in educational settings. Her primary contributions are works implementing the regulations for Title IX legislation, which provides for the equality of educational opportunity for females and males. Most prominent among these works are her three workshop packages: (1) "Implementing Title IX and Attaining Sex Equity: A Workshop Package for Elementary-Secondary Educators"; (2) "Complying with Title IX: A Resource Kit"; (3) "Program for Equity: Schools and Affirmative Action." In addition, Shirley and her associates have conducted "The First National Conference on Sex Role Stereotyping in Elementary and Secondary Education" and "The First National Conference on Sexism and Teacher Education."

For all of these activities, Shirley has received numerous awards, including the Human Relations Award from the National Education Association. Perhaps the most prominent indicator of performance is the fact that approximately 150,000 of these resource kits have been disseminated and are being used in school districts around the country. In sum, Shirley's works have set a standard of excellence for the implementation of all human equity programs.

Shirley's basic assumption about life is that each of us shares the responsibility for our own life and for the lives of others. She implements this assumption in her work for social change. Since she sees life in a more social, wholistic way, her sense of satisfaction comes in seeing others grow and achieve as well as in her own productivity and accomplishments.

At the same time, many people surrounding Shirley, colleagues and recipients as well as supervisors, do not understand the purity of her motives or the militancy of her pursuit. The crises in her life are often a consequence of this cynical reaction to her efforts. Typical is the resistance of the bureaucracy to the initiatives of the feminine constituency to claim their full rights as well as responsibilities. Since Shirley has made her supportive thrust intellectually substantive, she has often become a target of the bureaucracy. Consequently, they have withheld positions and promotions, thus denying career development; information, thus retarding data-based effectiveness; fair evaluations, thus misrepresenting the outcomes which the projects were intended to affect. Shirley has resolved these crises in the same way that she has resolved dying: " ... by attempting to ensure that my life made a positive difference and that some of my work will be reflected in the future development of others and in achieving social justice."

How Shirley actualizes her potential in implementing her mission can be seen in the profile in Figure 8–1. As can be seen, all of Shirley's ratings are at level 4.0 or above, thus describing a person closely approximating the actualization of her potential.

To others, Shirley has seemingly boundless energy. However, because she has only a periodic fitness program, she is limited to functioning with intensity. Although she has been open in taking

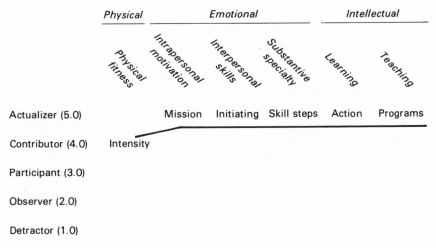

FIGURE 8-1 Actualization profile of McCune

on tasks that would be overwhelming for others, she has become increasingly aware of stamina limitations. It is precisely in the physical arena that the most dramatic and immediate effects of overall deterioration (or growth) may be experienced. Consequently, she invests herself selectively with intensity. Relatedly, Shirley is increasingly attuned to her need to take more time for herself in order to build herself physically. (Level 4.0—Physically)

Shirley's current motivations are clear to her although she is the first to acknowledge that people confuse personal ambitions with personal contributions: "We must be concerned about the good of society as well as our own personal advancement or reward." In this context, Shirley has developed cumulatively through the motivational levels: performing to receive the rewards of the incentive system; functioning to satisfy her own achievement ethic; work to fulfill herself within her own personal life space; committing herself to a mission outside of herself—a mission "to increase social justice and improve the achievement of others." At the same time, because of her overpowering schedule, she finds herself longing to spend more time in personal interests and pursuits in order to fill up all of the life space available to her. (Level 5.0—Emotivationally)

Interpersonally, Shirley is initially shy yet open and receptive. She is responsive to others and makes a great effort to help them personalize their goals and to initiate programs. In this regard, she attempts systematically to have regular contacts with people she cares for as well as for staff she is responsible for. She focuses upon gaining feedback from a variety of sources to further insure the sharpness of her interpersonal skills. (Level 5.0—Interpersonally)

Perhaps Shirley's greatest strength lies in her substantive specialty, which is social change interventions, primarily educational. With the acquisition of program development skills, she has operationalized her equity goals and technologized the means to these goals. She has continuously measured her level of expertise by her increased ability to deal with complexity which is reflected in her movement up her career ladder. (Level 5.0—Substantively)

In taking upon herself increasingly complex levels of responsibility, Shirley enters each new position as a very intense learner. Her approach to learning is quite cognitive. She explores the material written about her area in order to develop a deductive model for entry. She gets her hands dirty in acquiring first-hand information with which to modify her understanding and from which to develop data-based policies. She plans the action programs to achieve the goals of her policies. (Level 5.0—Learning)

Perhaps Shirley has as much experience in teaching as in any other area. She has taught women in every state of the union to implement her programs for achieving equity. Indeed, she has been extremely strong and sensitive in preparing her content, diagnosing her recipients, and helping them set and achieve goals. (Level 5.0—Teaching)

In summary, Shirley functions modally at Level 5.0, with only her physical fitness serving to limit the degree to which she actualizes her resources (Level 4.0). Her motivational mission is clear and unmistaken and outside of herself in achieving the hopes and ambitions of the disenfranchised peoples of this world. Her interpersonal initiative is efficient and effective, Shirley being able to facilitate people movement directly toward a personalized course of action. She can operationalize all goals and technologize all programs in her substantive specialty yet maintains an open learning system for increasingly complex levels of input and increasingly focused products of output. Her teaching programs set standards of excellence for all social change programs.

Although Shirley got her initial impetus from the disparity in treatment of males and females, she is humble with herself, seeing herself primarily as an honest worker who is absorbed and involved in her work. While the lack of a continuous fitness program places possible limits upon her enormous constitutional resources, Shirley has within her grasp the actualization of her physical, emotional, and intellectual resources. What is required is a pacing program that will allow her to survive the preliminary events in order to function fully in the forthcoming main events of her life.

David N. Aspy

David N. Aspy was a poor boy, born in rural Kentucky, the second of three brothers. His father was a pistol-toting, labor-organizing, Southern Baptist preacher; his mother a bible-toting, homemaking, preacher's wife. Dave distinguished himself early by his athletic and singing ability. Although he went to college on an athletic scholarship, it was only after he was exposed to the teachings of elite scientists at the University of Chicago while he was in military service that he started to realize the vast parameters of the world and his opportunity to contribute within them. After a career in teaching, coaching, and counseling, Dave became involved in studying the effective ingredients of education. This pursuit culminated years later in the development by him and his associates of The National Consortium for Humanizing Education—a consortium of hundreds of school systems emphasizing the training of teachers in interpersonal and other teaching skills. The results of his work have been summarized most recently in a highly acclaimed book called *KIDS Don't Learn from People They Don't Like.*

Dave's work has been reviewed in print by distinguished educators possessing the highest credentials. Carl Rogers of the *Center for the Study of the Person* has been laudatory: "For a number of years, Aspy has been the leader in a series of research studies aimed at finding out whether human, person-centered characteristics in a classroom have any measurable effects; and, if so, what these effects are.... No study of comparable magnitude has ever been made...."

Howard Kirschenbaum, co-director of the National Humanistic Education Center, concluded in his review of work in the *First Catalogue for Humanizing Education* that "David Aspy is probably the leading person in this country doing rigorous research on the techniques and concepts of humanistic education."

James W. Becker of the *National Foundation for the Improvement of Education* has stated, "This book will be the cornerstone for tomorrow's educational systems. Aspy and Roebuck have succeeded in maintaining the principles of scientific investigation under the most difficult conditions." In sum, Aspy has received the highest reviews from scholars of demonstrated expertise in Aspy's substantive specialty.

Dave's basic assumption about life is that it is a gift and should be used productively for one's own growth as well as the growth of others. In his daily living, he tries to implement this assumption by monitoring his own behavior. He has a personal confrontation every day concerning what he is doing with this precious gift of life. He has found that many people pull away from having this same question imposed upon them implicitly by his presence. Dave has resolved dying because he knows in his being there is an eternal life. "The next breath you take will be in heaven."

Characteristically, Dave has managed the crises in his life in accordance with his values. When he was "thrown out" of a graduate psychology program for doing things that helped people rather than experimenting with them; when he resigned along with other staff because of the inordinate pressures put upon them in creating an entirely new orientation to helping and teaching; when an entire department voted against him in his pursuit of humanizing education; when he was dislodged from his efforts to work at a small black college; when he struggled for life before and after heart surgery—in all of these instances and more—Dave never lost sight of his mission. He used crises to sharpen his values, to make a more profound commitment to his mission, and to become more selective about his investments and the people with whom he has shared.

In this context, Dave's only reason for living is now profoundly spiritual. How Dave actualizes his potential in carrying forward this fundamental value is seen in the profile in Figure 8-2. As can be seen, all of Dave's ratings are at level 4.0 or above, thus describing a person moving toward actualizing his human potential.

Dave had an extraordinarily strong start physically, however, he suffered a setback in his late forties with a hereditary heart disease. Open heart surgery was required. Now in his early fifties, Dave

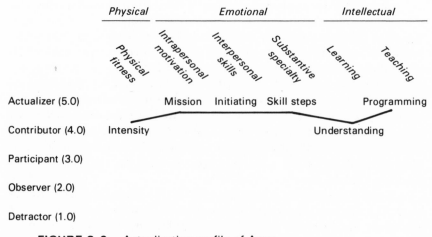

FIGURE 8-2 Actualization profile of Aspy

continues a 5-to-6 mile-per-day jogging-walking program. He monitors himself semiannually on the stress test, which involves 22 minutes on the treadmill. The tests indicate results in the range of those of professional athletes. Nevertheless, Dave is cognizant of stamina limitations and invests himself intensively now in efforts on a selective basis (Level 4.0—Physically).

Emotivationally, Dave was conditioned to a sense of mission by his early religious training. After working through the developmental levels of motivation, Dave has again acquired a sense of mission in his commitment to humankind. His nontraditional career reflects choices valuing this mission over his personal career development or even over his own personal fulfillment. Currently, he sees his personal fulfillment in striving to be a "magnificent human being," as close to perfection as is humanly "possible." This attitude emphasizes his real mission of facilitating the efforts of those people who can impact the world constructively (Level 5.0—Emotivationally).

Interpersonally, Dave's interest is in humankind in general. He can be observed relating accurately to others' frames of reference in all interactions. Where appropriate, he can help others to personalize goals and initiate action programs. He sees himself as striving to open up to all peoples and to be known by all peoples at all levels of humanity, especially the spiritual. He feels that he knows what he wants to do because he has received at the highest levels but feels that he has not yet given himself at the highest levels: "Then shall I know even as also I am known" (Level 5.0—Interpersonally).

Dave has devoted his life to educating children and educators of children. His products reflect not only goal specification but detailed steps for teachers implementing interpersonal and cognitive skills in the classroom. In the process of refining his programs, he and his associates have listened to more than fifty thousand hours of classroom teaching and have based their programs on what they have learned from evaluating the effects of teaching upon thousands of school children. Above all, Dave is an operationalizer of teaching and learning goals and a technologizer of teaching and learning deliveries. His teacher-training methods are detailed in atomistic steps that teachers have received and used with their learners (Level 5.0—Substantively).

Dave is himself a kinesthetic learner, a learning style emphasized by poor children; thus perhaps, the identification with affecting their opportunities to learn. Currently, he has two learning tasks: (1) to help create a Christian technology, a way of providing the skills needed to achieve the humanistic purposes of Christianity; (2) to conquer the dimensions of the political arena to facilitate the translations from productivity to political power. At this time, his goals are clear but his action programs to accomplish them are not yet delineated. (This state is common upon entry into a new area of endeavor.) (Level 4.0—Learning)

Dave's track record in teaching reflects an enormously successful effort in reaching thousands of teachers in hundreds of different school systems around the world. To accomplish this tremendous effort, Dave and his associates have developed detailed teaching delivery programs that communicate with a wide diversity of audiences. His teaching goal is to give as much as he can for as long as he can to free people to make their contributions. While he is currently engaged in improving his ability to process and communicate information, he is already a magnificent teacher, as measured by all criteria, including some which he helped to develop (Level 5.0— Teaching).

As can be seen, Dave functions modally somewhere approaching actualization (approaching Level 5.0—Overall). Whereas his heart condition places a lid on his stamina, he still functions with great intensity in appropriate areas. His mission is clearly defined and outside of himself, defining "becoming magnificent" as facilitating the contributions of others. Interpersonally, he is able to personalize goals and initiate the development of action programs with others. He has developed his substantive specialty to the atomistic steps necessary to affect target behavior. His own ongoing learning programs are developed at the level of understanding the goals and are moving toward developing the action programs to get to the goals. His teaching programs are broken down into the content, lesson plans, and teaching methods necessary to individualize learners' programs.

Whereas Dave got his initial impetus from his tremendous physical energy and his emotional commitment, with a lid placed upon his physical development, Dave realizes that he must compensate with still higher levels of intellectual development. Foremost in his mind is developing the substantive dimensions of a Christian technology that can be applied in the arenas of politics and policy, just as he developed and applied teacher training programs. He then can bring his own learning programs to the action phase and build his teaching programs to communicate his actions. Dave's own conclusion summarizes this principle: "The only reason for living is to discover and use your reason to implement your reason for being."

Andrew H. Griffin, Jr.

Andrew H. Griffin, Jr. was a poor black boy, born in the inner-city of Springfield, Massachusetts, the sixth oldest of seventeen children. His father worked two jobs to support his family, and his mother spent long days, as she has throughout her life, providing the physical and psychological nourishment to a family that now includes more than sixty grandchildren. Andy, as he is now known to his professional colleagues, will always be "Bootsie" to the family from whom he has both drawn and given responsive strength and initiative support:

> The role that my Mother and Father have played in my life. I come from a family of seventeen and had no idea or thought of being poor until I went to college and they talked about poverty levels according to income and number of people in a family. I was taught to believe that no one was better than I. Nor I better than anyone else. They taught us to recognize opportunity and that everyone should be given the same opportunity. They allowed us to be individuals but demanded us to be the best, as well as be able to accept the consequences for whatever we did. My mother tended to be understanding and demanding. My father tended to be demanding and understanding. Both my mother and father were very, very strong and had a 360-degree reinforcement program in all the areas they believed. They loved and fought violently. It was an "either-or" world. You did or you didn't. It was very easy for me to understand that. They accepted all people, regardless of race, and allowed you to join or participate in all constructive activities. My sisters could play baseball and basketball equal to my brothers and myself. Thus, the idea of sexism was foreign to me. Although I recognized the difference in color, it was really the capabilities of a person that received the attention.
>
> My mother and father sat upon my shoulders many times when I was about to make a major decision. More often than not my behavior was influenced by what I thought they would have done. It is still from this background I draw much of my thinking regardless of what the research or renowned person says. It is from my early experience in life with my mother and father that provided me with the foundation for later life. Whatever I did, whether I felt comfortable or not, they were concerned that I did it with the best of my energies. Because my mother was able to remain home, I knew that I was able to reach her at any time. I believe psychologically and realistically this provided me with a genuine support system. Further, my father constantly assessed and challenged me in all the activities that I became a part of, including leading demonstrations which he did not fully appreciate.

As he began to mature, Andy distinguished himself athletically. Starring in college football, he later played professionally. After laboring in many menial positions to support his undergraduate education, Andy became first a teacher and then director of a large tutorial service for poor Black, Brown, and White youth. While these experiences provided great emotional and intellectual growth, however, what really facilitated the explosion of his growth was his experience as co-director of a Center for Human Relations and Community Affairs established by a small college to service the inner-city population that surrounded it:

> This experience allowed me to use and develop my talents and skills as well. The people working with me served as mentors as well as my students. It was a sharing experience. The focus on the developing and the acquisition of skills helped me to recognize that I had a host of skills and that people need skills to increase their effectiveness. Further, the experience provided me with a tool to help people understand and expand themselves. It also gave me the opportunity to understand society at a deeper level. The people with whom I was in contact were very effective and the type I wanted my children to emulate. With this backdrop, "Ain't No Stopping Me Now."

These growth experiences have enabled Andy to climb the ladder of career achievement, through a Harvard doctorate to a research manager position in the National Education Association. In the process, he has been instrumental in producing products concerned with his mission in life, what he terms "multicultural sex equity." He is the author of *Beyond Uniculturalism,* co-author with George Banks and Patricia Benivedez of a series on *Multicultural Education,* and has been the guiding force in the development of a *Women's Leadership Training* package. Dr. Bernard G. Berenson, noted social scientist and former associate, says of Dr. Griffin's work: "No one in the history of the world has thought more inclusively about humankind and developed more operationally the goal of fulfilling human potential for all peoples everywhere."

Andy's basic assumption about life is that life is a very special gift: "People try to avoid work. They tend to think they are the beginning and the end of the world. Life is beautiful. Everything is achievable. People want to maintain the status quo. Everyone wants to be liked and respected and they want to give. Most people don't want to be different. Everyone can grow and contribute. My basic assumption is that you're either constructive or destructive. We want our children to be effective and as constructive as possible. I try to live my life as constructive as possible."

Andy implements these assumptions by being a mature model, by "looking for teachable moments, providing multicultural experiences whenever the opportunity arises." He always tries to understand and communicate his understanding to others, "to go beyond the parameters, to not be locked in by a job—it should not control your principles."

Andy has resolved dying by living: "I don't worry about it. When it happens, it happens." In this same characteristic manner, he deals with the crises in his life, unraveling the problem, finding the life threads and weaving them into a beautiful, growing, changing pattern. The people around him, he finds, evidence reactions of openness and positiveness on the one hand; curiosity, uncertainty, puzzlement in the middle; and fearfulness and undermining, hostile behavior on the other hand. He relates to these responses simply and differentially by assisting those who strive for life, observing those who are struggling, and cutting free of those who are retarding life development in themselves and others.

In a self-contained and inner-directed manner, Andy relates to himself in a similar rigorous manner—positively reinforcing his own growth impulses; vigilantly observing himself where his impulses are in question; extinguishing his own nongrowth impulses. Consequently, as can be seen in Figure 8-3, Andy approaches functioning at Level 5.0 across all indices of human potential.

Physically, Andy is an extremely vigorous forty-five-year-old, maintaining a physical fitness program for both endurance and in-

	Physical	Emotional			Intellectual	
	Physical fitness	Intrapersonal motivation	Interpersonal skills	Substantive specialty	Learning	Teaching
Actualizer (5.0)	Stamina	Mission	Initiating	Skill steps	Action	Program
Contributor (4.0)						
Participant (3.0)						
Observer (2.0)						
Detractor (1.0)						

FIGURE 8-3 Actualization profile of Griffin

tensity. He has clear physical goals, including running a less-than-eight-minute mile regularly, along with 150 sit-ups and 50 push-ups and 1,000 consecutive jumps with the jump rope, plus recreational jogging, bowling, and swimming and competitive tennis and basketball. His enormous energy reservoir allows him to function with great intensity for long hours with very little sleep (Level 5.0—Physically).

Emotivationally, Andy draws great strength from his mission of "multicultural sex equity" or "helping the disenfranchised people of the world to realize their full potential." Andy has seen himself work through the different levels of motivation because he has been surrounded by people who were always demanding the next level of development from themselves. He is constantly recognizing his weaknesses and realigning them to better serve his mission in life (Level 5.0—Emotivationally).

Part and parcel of his commitment, then, is Andy's commitment to expanding his own humanity by entering the frames of reference of others and incorporating their constructive dimensions in his inclusive mission. Accordingly, he lives in an intensely reciprocating cycle of interdependency with those around him, "understanding and being understood, building together upon each other's frameworks, and identifying goals and strategies to achieve these goals" (Level 5.0—Interpersonally).

Intellectually, Andy's substantive specialty involves employing an interpersonal skills vehicle to multicultural education. He measures his level of expertise by the feedback he receives on his ability to move people from one level of development to another. He technologizes the means to his own goals by developing technical programs, writing technical papers, and training people to be able to replicate and build upon the techniques to achieve their own goals (Level 5.0—Substantively).

In terms of learning, Andy is perhaps at his strongest. His entire being is focused upon observing and listening to others; analyzing, synthesizing, and operationalizing the content of their expressions; and technologizing the means to achieve the worthwhile goals embodied in those expressions. Part of this process involves diagnosing himself, identifying skills in areas that are not part of his response repertoire at the present time, and seeking avenues to gain those skills (Level 5.0—Learning).

Andy's teaching directly reflects his learning. Indeed, his teaching is a shared, teaching-learning process. Accordingly, he is constantly comparing his ability to his students' abilities and consequently expanding his response repertoire in helping all persons to learn more effectively. He is at his dramatic best in motivating the learners and in delivering his systematic skills program to them (Level 5.0—Teaching).

As can be seen, then, Andy functions modally at Level 5.0 overall: physically with intensity and endurance; emotivationally with a clear life mission; interpersonally with responsiveness and initiative; substantively with operational goals and technical steps to achieve them; in learning and teaching with systematic programs. Clearly, Andy got his impetus from his enormous constitution and his nurturant environment and his stimulating colleagues. He gives payment for these gifts by attempting to be the most effective person he can be and by helping others to become the most effective people they can be. Effectiveness is his most important value. He uses it to guide his important life decisions: "Is it constructive? Is it challenging? Will it help others? Will it increase my opportunity to influence more people? Will it increase my responsibility?"

SOME NOTES ON ACTUALIZERS

One of the characteristics that distinguishes actualizers from non-actualizers is the child-like innocence they exhibit in their disposition toward learning. They appear unafraid of experiences that their more cynical counterparts have long since retreated from. They really want to know the answers to questions; they truly want to know whether something can be done.

This apparent innocence is not the innocence of the immature child who thinks he or she can live forever. Actualizers know they can be killed physically and with this knowledge comes the loss of innocence. Still they have chosen to live their lives as though they were innocent. Because for them it would not be worthwhile to live their lives at all if every decision were based upon the fear of death, whether psychological or physical.

Accordingly, actualizers live their lives as if they were not afraid. They fear no punishment from their superiors or subordinates or any of a range of people with whom they become involved. They choose positions that others refuse or abandon careers to serve a mission. This does not mean that they do not experience hurt and pain. It also does not mean that they have insulated themselves against the intensity of these experiences. Quite the contrary! They know that in their intense moments they may experience more attack in a day than others will in a lifetime. They know that the same walls that are built to prevent hurt also prevent growth. They know that experiences of all kinds are the richest source of growth.

Typically, actualizers experience the hurtful as well as the helpful and loving experiences at the very deepest and most intense levels possible. But they do not linger along with these experiences. They mourn a loss and celebrate a find fully in the moment. Although their experiences are cumulative in terms of their learning, actualizers do not dominate existential experiences with lingering remnants of historical feelings.

In this context, actualizers are not shaped by conventional incentives. Indeed, as Kipling suggests, they tend to treat the "twin imposters" of triumph and defeat in the very same manner. They are concerned only with their own objective assessments of their own calculated movement toward their objectives. Perhaps most important in relation to their experiences, they use their experiences as a source of developing courses of action.

Not unrelatedly, actualizers have a tendency to employ straightforward logic and move directly toward their goals and objectives. This course often leads to servicing directly the intended recipients of their programs, an approach that frequently runs counter to the bureaucratic policies of business and government. There, people who find no intrinsic fulfillment in their work are dominated thoroughly by the career development factor that is controlled by their superiors. There is a direct conflict for the non-actualizer who is oriented "up" and the actualizer who is oriented "down." Often the actualizer is the apparent loser in the career game but the winner in terms of producing constructive outcomes. If the actualizer chooses to play again the career game in another setting, he or she will be eminently more effective in doing so because of the accumulation of these performance indicators.

It is not at all that the actualizers cannot identify with superiors as well as peers and subordinates. It is simply that they can only be certain of the justice they create in the realms they control. They are entirely identified with rational leadership and quite capable of compromise, so long as the steps of compromise take them closer to the goals and objectives of the missions they serve.

In conclusion, while non-actualizers are constricting throughout life, actualizers are constructing throughout life. For non-actualizers physical death is only symbolic. They died years earlier when they fled from the challenge of their first crisis and resolved not to enter the unknown. They live dying.

Actualizers view dying physically as a new learning experience. They do not retreat from the challenges of life. And, in the end, they die growing.

V
The context of
actualizing

9
Assumptions and implications

Perhaps the best way to begin a clinical study of the assumptions of people who are in the process of actualizing themselves is with a view of facing death. We all wonder how we will face death someday. Here is the story of how one of the persons concerned with actualizing faced that moment.

When I went into cancer surgery, I did not know what the outcome would be. I took along some books on systems development. Simply because that was what I was studying at the moment. As I was wheeled into surgery, I remember engaging in conversation with the interns and residents about the twin passions of my life, the human's use of his or her intellect in the pursuit of social justice. The last thing that I can remember as I went under was trying to deal with a question which one of the young physicians put to me—concerning her making her contributions more effectively. I have since reflected upon a personal entry which I made in my intellectual journal prior to surgery.

"I don't know what my chances are. The data says one-out-of-three survive. My physician says that since I am physically strong and emotionally 'together', my chances are good. If I can add an

intellectual dimension concerning my will power, then I would agree.

"But this is not something that I will control as I have created my life. I have made my life as productive as possible. I plan to use whatever time I have left—whether months or years—as productively as possible.

"I do not view my affliction with sadness. Nor do I experience anger or fear. Or ask the question, 'Why me?' Why not me? I feel only happiness and fullness for the privilege of having lived in my time and place. I feel no great sense of urgency to intensify my efforts to contribute. Only a sense of continuing.

"In a very real way, I view this crisis just as I have viewed every other crisis in my life: as an opportunity to grow—perhaps not physically, but certainly emotionally and intellectually. Certainly, it is possible to die growing in mind and soul.

"I will also use this as an opportunity to reflect upon the meaning of life. It would be neurotic to do otherwise."

These excerpts typify the outlook of one actualizer—a kind of simultaneous immediacy of experiencing and awareness of processes converging upon the phenomenon in the moment. Dying from unavoidable causes is really no big thing. As one actualizer said, "Dying is part of living—if you resolve living, you resolve dying."

ASSUMPTIONS

Perhaps the most important thing that we can know about actualizers is how they resolve living. We can learn much from understanding the assumption they make about life. The most important assumption they make universally revolves around the relationship between life and growth. It may be represented as follows (see Figure 9–1):

Life is growth

It follows from this basic assumption that the only reason to live is to grow—to fulfill one's potential; to actualize one's physical, emotional, and intellectual resources. For an actualizer, the process of growth "is the actualization of the gift of life."

Developmentally, they first apply this assumption to themselves. They set about to dedicate their lives to growing. They, then,

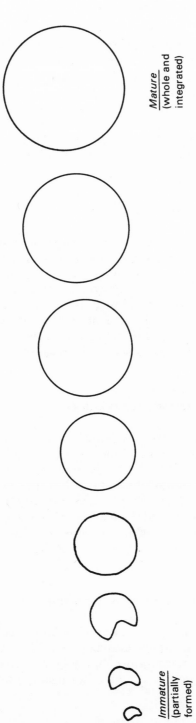

Immature
(partially
formed)

Mature
(whole and
integrated)

Figure 9-1   Life is growth

realize that others also deserve the opportunity to grow. At this point, they develop some kind of mission in life that involves providing the opportunity for others to grow.

There are a number of corollaries that flow from this fundamental assumption about life. These corollaries represent the unique phenomenological experience of actualizers. The corollaries may be presented in a developmental manner to reflect the growth process for humans striving to be fully functioning.

Growth is wholeness

Initially, an actualizer seeks to become whole within himself or herself. That is to say, to develop and integrate resources on the broadest possible basis. In some instances, actualizers set out early in life to develop strengths in the area of their weaknesses so that they can serve their missions in life. In one case, a scholar who has since become known as one of the most prominent researchers of all time set out to compensate for his lack of knowledge and expertise in research. He continues to serve his mission.

Growth is expanding wholeness

In process, the persons struggling for fullness expand this wholeness in interaction with others in their worlds. By entering the frames of reference of others, gradually they incorporate more and more of the dimensions of others within themselves. In at least one instance, an actualizer set out systematically to encounter people of different cultures around the world—not only to expand the boundaries of his humanity but also to look for "the constant threads in human experience."

Growth is expanding to become one with the world

Ultimately, actualizers expand their wholeness to incorporate all of the dimensions of others and their worlds. In so doing, they incorporate their own humanity "for what is each of us but a part of all of us." Perhaps the words of one of the people studied are appropriate here:

If any of my brothers or sisters live in poverty, so also am I poor.

If any of my brothers or sisters are addicted, so also am I addicted.

If any of my brothers or sisters are convicted as criminals, so also am I convicted as a criminal.

If any of my brothers or sisters are imprisoned, so also am I imprisoned.

In actuality, there is no ultimate in functioning for the self-actualizing person. The world is always expanding as the people within it expand their own humanity. Actualizers are always expanding to search out the boundaries of themselves and their worlds.

In the human end, for there is no real end, the fully functioning person transmits vitality to others in an ongoing attempt to facilitate the actualizing process for others in their worlds. Actualizers leave their lives with people equipped to actualize their own potential as well as that of the institutions of their worlds.

IMPLICATIONS

If we can understand the assumptions underlying a particular approach or orientation, then we can calculate the implications. Indeed, this is one of the functions at which actualizers distinguish themselves—describing, predicting, and thus creating their worlds. If the system is logical, the assumptions dictate the implications.

Thus, if life is growth, then a growth system must be set up to facilitate the actualization of growth potential. If life is found in subjective experience and objective reality, the growth system must be set up to input, process, and output both experiential and informational data. The process by which we expand our human dimensions becomes both the means and the ends of life.

Growing is the means and ends of life

If growing is the means and ends of life, then the mechanisms of learning both require and reflect a multidimensional person. The person must incorporate all of the dimensions needed to receive, process, and produce data. The person must use this data to develop his or her physical, emotional, and intellectual resources and to develop and apply skills in living, learning, and working arenas.

Growing is multidimensional development

Further, if growing is reflected in multidimensional development, then all dimensions within the person are interdependent (see Figure 9–2). That is, the effects upon any one dimension affect all other dimensions directly and indirectly. All systems, both within and between people and their worlds, interact. We are all dependent upon each other and our worlds.

Growing is interdependent systems development

We all exist on a fragile spacecraft called "Earth" only by the grace of forces much greater than ours. Life is, after all, but a precious, fleeting glimpse of our oneness with eternity. It is this oneness with eternal life that actualizers ultimately experience.

REACTIONS AND LIABILITIES

There is a whole other set of implications that may be derived from the assumptions actualizers make about life. These are the responses of other people. Because actualizers believe the life assumptions and their implications are profound does not mean they will be rewarded for attempts to actualize potential. "In the land of the blind, the one-eyed man is not king and the two-eyed man is the enemy" (Aspy, 1971). Internal growth and the assumption of the responsibilities it implies is, itself, reward and sufficient to overcome any external punishments.

There are two fundamental sets of responses to the assumptions of the fully functioning person. The first may be termed the growth action. The second may be termed the nongrowth reaction.

Growth action

In the growth response, the actor emulates the dimensions of the fully functioning person. For example, the actor functioning adequately on responsiveness may act to sharpen the accuracy of his or her responsiveness as well as to learn to develop action initiatives. Similarly, the actor functioning adequately on initiative may act to operationalize the programs of his or her initiatives as well as to learn to respond sensitively to people in the environment.

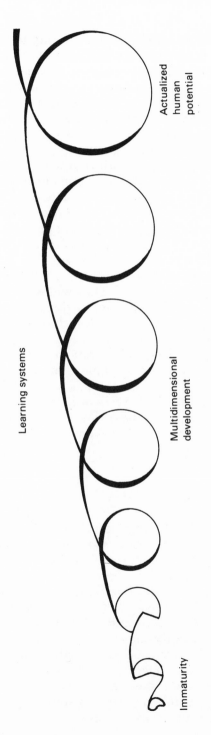

Figure 9-2 Growing is interdependent systems development

If the actors have a picture or a diagnostic chart available, they may, in effect, plot or diagnose themselves with regard to their levels of functioning on a variety of dimensions—or they may take the exploratory inventory. Building upon their strengths, they may learn to develop goals for functioning effectively in their areas of weakness. They can develop systematic programs to reinforce and sharpen their strengths as well as to acquire the skills and knowledge required to be fully functioning.

Thus, the actors may utilize actualizers as their models for their own personal growth and development. If they are fortunate, they may also receive the skills of the actualizers as the agents of their growth. Here, they should be reminded of the cost-benefit nature of the investments of fully functioning persons: They will only invest where there is an incrementally greater return. It is as if each of them were climbing a mountain. They will only pull on the ropes of those tied to them. They occasionally will help those who slip but only if they pull their own weight. They will work diligently to save those who save others. They will cut the lines of those who only drag upon the line—which is no more nor less than they would do to themselves in the same situation. For in the end, actualizers universally recognize that it is more important that one person grow to his or her fullest than it is for all other people to muddle their ways through life. One of the actualizers' missions is to pass on the love of life—in all of its truth, beauty, and excellence. Without their growing existence, the next generation would be lost and lonely, at best conditioned to be responsive or initiative; at worst, passively engaged in destroying itself cell by cell.

Nongrowth reactions

The paths of actualizers, while often difficult, are the only ones they can take, for to do otherwise is to shortchange themselves. They see the other choice daily in the obstacles developed by less than fully functioning people. They recognize that, while they are the non-actualizers' only alternative, non-actualizers constitute no option at all for them. They live on qualitatively different planes that are quantum leaps in spirit and practice from others.

There are many images that we can conjure up of the reactions to actualizers. Let this be simply said: Non-actualizers know immediately when they meet actualizers just as the actualizers know immediately when they meet non-actualizers. However, where actualizers are tolerant of non-actualizers, non-actualizers are totally intolerant of actualizers.

The most potent of non-actualizers are people who at the peak of their lives physically may have the energy reservoirs based upon their youth and physical activities. However, they gradually dissipate their energy reservoir and reduce themselves to physically surviving each day. Again, at their peaks emotionally, they may have a high need to achieve but gradually this gives way to orienting themselves around the incentive system. Similarly, at their peaks interpersonally they may be responsive to the frames of reference of other people. However, because they never are concerned or skilled enough to follow through in personalizing goals and individualizing programs to achieve the goals, they never really learn anything. Gradually they become less and less responsive and finally less and less attentive. The same atrophy occurs in the intellectual areas. Above all, non-actualizers are nonsubstantive people. While they may develop a few principles early on in their careers, they gradually regress to the concept level, often forgetting all but their most basic principles. Although they are sometimes experts at exploring in learning ("the divergent producers"), and diagnosing in teaching ("the screening experts"), they slowly cease to be because they never carry anything to culmination: They never really learn or teach for the rest of their lives.

The problem is that non-actualizers peak early in their lives. Their marriages are at their heights on the wedding night. Their children are "best" when they are young. Their learning is best in the first moments. Their careers peak in their late twenties and early thirties. And it is downhill thereafter. In their late thirties they are beginning to plan for retirement—we may ask, "Retirement from what?" At the same time, they are becoming restless, seeking to "cash in" on their positions with the best houses, cars, clothes, dinners, and members of the opposite sex. In their forties, they are already looking for ways to "bail-out" early. Some ways involve large gambles like making the "big kill" in investments—they are always on the verge of doing so. Others are more devious. Their behavior becomes frenetic and then frantic as their fantasies entitle them to everything and reality delivers them nothing. There is not even a memory trace of the growth potential to which they were once really entitled but refused.

Then, they meet the actualizers—the people who chose what they refused but can no longer remember. The actualizers stand as living confrontation to non-actualizers: They represent what non-actualizers might have been had they had the courage to withstand people like themselves. The non-actualizer's reaction is immediate: The actualizers are someone they can never be. The actualizers are going to move on beyond the current settings. In work settings, they are going to acquire the performance indicators that will enable them to move to new and higher level jobs (whether or not they take the jobs has to do with the job's consistency with the actualizer's mission). At the same time, the non-actualizers will be passed over with increasing frequency: Thus, by their own criteria they fail to compete effectively with people who value other criteria. Even where the non-actualizer is boss, he or she must work to neutralize the thrust of the actualizer. It is as if, upon meeting, the non-actualizer is aware of the actualizer's potential destiny—even more so than the actualizer who is simply working to fulfill every moment of his or her existence. For the actualizer, it is fruitless to try to develop or restore a communication process that never was with a person who does not exist. It is far better for the actualizers to recognize the non-actualizers for what they are—retarders and destroyers of others' potential—and to feign the communication that their adversaries deserve. In the end, in spite of everything the non-actualizers do, the actualizers, if they are true to their missions, will fulfill their own potential and their destiny. By working in the present, the actualizers fulfill the non-actualizer's fantasies.

TOWARD ACTUALIZING SELF-ACTUALIZATION

The issue of achieving self-actualization is a question of motivation: How do we motivate people to become more than they are? Experientially, we all tend to think that we are functioning adequately so long as we see people around us who are relatively poorer in functioning. It is only when we experience someone who is functioning at higher levels that we suspect we may be cheating ourselves. Even then, we are reluctant to invest ourselves without assurances that we can make it to the higher level.

There are, then, at least three conditions for achieving self-actualization: (1) one's awareness of a model for a high level of functioning; (2) the experience of the discrepancy in functioning between oneself and the model; (3) a didactic teaching program to close the gap in functioning. These are the ingredients of achieving self-actualization: modeling, experiential, and didactic.

The first condition relates to the model that the first person presents for a high level of functioning. The model must be seen as an effective way of functioning in absolute terms. Both its process and its benefits must be clear to the perceiver.

The second condition relates to the experience of the relative discrepancy between the first and second person's level of functioning. The first person must either be functioning within a level of the second person or must present himself or herself as functioning within a level. The second person must experience the discrepancy but not in an overwhelmingly unachievable way.

The third condition relates to the didactic teaching program that can be employed to close the gap between the first and second person. This didactic program must be broken out in such a way as to insure the success of the second person in seeking to function at a higher level.

In effect, the second person experiences the benefits produced by the first person's way of life; experiences himself or herself as being cheated of significant meaning in life; experiences the opportunity to achieve a higher level of functioning with safety.

When any of these conditions are not met, the second person fails to move to the higher level of functioning. If the first person is experienced as functioning at too high a level or the discrepancy is experienced as too great or the program is not systematic enough, then the second person will fail to move to the next level of functioning.

If there is no helper around to meet these conditions, the person must help or teach himself or herself—estimating the beneficial process and outcomes of the first person, diagnosing the discrepancy between levels of functioning, setting and operationalizing goals, technologizing the means to achieve these goals. Where the second person does not have the expertise, he or she must search for it in the form of people or materials.

There is evidence from our work in interpersonal skills to suggest that the second person's gain in functioning will be a consequence of the discrepancy between the first and second person's functioning (Carkhuff, 1969). In general, with intensive and extensive contacts, the helpee/trainee moves toward the helper/trainer's level of functioning. In the process, the helpees gain about one-half the discrepancy in functioning (see Table 9-1). This means that the helper must be functioning at a relatively high level of functioning for the helpee to benefit. If the helper is relatively neutral, the benefits will be neutralized. If the helper is relatively low, the consequences will be retarding for the helpee.

In summary, the fully functioning person is totally aware that any significant human relationship is in the process of deepening or deteriorating. Stability in any relationship is only an illusion. When a relationship is not growing, it undergoes changes that increase distance between those involved. This fact holds true for parent-child, teacher-student, husband-wife, and helper-helpee relationships.

TABLE 9-1 Formula for the effects of training upon level of trainee functioning

TRAINEE CHANGE
IN LEVEL OF   =   1/2 Initial level   −   1/2 Initial level   +
FUNCTIONING   of trainer   of trainee
                    functioning   functioning

1/20 Discrepancy   0.2
      between initial + (a constant)
      levels

The self-actualizing person is resigned to facing the implications of being a step ahead or above most of those with whom he or she comes in contact. Knowing when not to act or to respond in terms of his or her deep sensitivities requires fine discriminations. These actions depend upon whether or not the second person recognizes that the fully functioning person can be a positive and constructive influence; that is, whether the second person cedes the power in the relationship to the self-actualizing person.

Following cancer surgery, when the patient returned for the results of the medical analysis, he was informed that there was no evidence of any "residual melanoma." In other words, no current signs of cancer. Even in a situation awaiting a life or death announcement, he responded to the physician's experience while being simultaneously and immediately aware of his own. He responded to the inhibited style of the physician's presentation, a style based upon defensively restricting involvement with patients whose chances of surviving are one in three.

"It's a happy occasion for you to bring good news to a patient. You don't always get that opportunity."

And they both smiled broadly and fully.

REFERENCES

Aspy, D. N. Forward. *The Development of Human Resources*. New York: Holt, Rinehart and Winston, 1971.

Carkhuff, R. R. *Helping and Human Relations*. New York: Holt, Rinehart and Winston, 1969.

Carkhuff, R. R. and Berenson, B. G. *Beyond Counseling and Therapy*. New York: Holt, Rinehart and Winston, 1967, 1977.

10
Marginality and variability

Once we had determined the dimensions of effectiveness in the helping and teaching professions, we set out to study the effects of graduate training upon these dimensions. To our dismay, we found that graduate training programs effectively eliminate those people functioning highest and lowest on these dimensions. The best and the worst are gone. What is left is the vast horde in the middle—those who cannot conceivably make a difference in the lives of others because they do not make a difference in their own lives.

Upon reflection, we now recognize that this finding is not unusual: For what is graduate training if it is not an analogue of society, eliminating its most marginal peoples—those who under different circumstances would become the leaders and contributors to the benefit of society.

One of the most interesting findings concerning actualizers is the nature of their marginality. In relation to the society in which they exist, they tend to be marginal persons. That is, whether they choose to be or not, they are seen as "different" and out of the "mainstream" or affairs. Indeed, they are way out on the edge of things. This position gives them a unique perspective of society and its phenomena. Because they see things differently from their perspectives, they tend to do different things with what they perceive: They discover dimensions that others could not see; they integrate processes that others thought disparate; they produce creative products that others could not conceive. For example, foremost among the persons who had the greatest impact upon Western society in the last century were Jews who existed on the margin of a Christian world—Einstein in science and technology, Freud in medicine and psychological treatment, and Marx in politics and government.

Because of their marginality, actualizers are creative leaders. Because of their creativity, they become the catalysts of change in their societies. Their potency and creativity attract some number of people within a given sphere of society and alter the random path of this vast amoebic institution we call society. Consequently, society moves toward the actualizers—not out of respect for their contribution but to incorporate their thrust and neutralize their threat. Thus, the society of science—indeed, the entire world—has reverberated around Einstein's theory of relativity and his applications in atomic technology. The societies of medicine and education have moved toward incorporating theories and treatment procedures reflecting Freud's view of the intrapsychic experiences of humankind. The societies of politics and government have revolved around Marxian concerns for justice for the poor and the needy.

In the moment, then, marginal people are seen as liabilities by the society that moves to isolate and eliminate them. The great irony is that if society is successful in eliminating them, it loses what it needs most—the increased diversity of perspectives in wrestling with its problems and achieving its goals. Conversely, if society is not successful in eliminating its marginal peoples, it wins. For in the end, the marginal peoples serve to move entire societies toward becoming more variable in relative terms and more healthy in absolute terms on all the dimensions of human resource development (Berenson, 1978).

In this context, it is no wonder that each succeeding wave of emigrants to the United States has—given a free public education system—produced the next wave of creative contributors within this country. Their physical energies are only one generation removed from the soil; they are motivated to become something more than the peasants their parents were; their intellects are poised to see things in sharp relief from their unique perspectives. With this recognition, it is great wonder why the next logical wave of contributors in American society—its own *Black and Brown* American migrants—are denied the opportunity to make their full contribution. Further, it is ironical that such great discrimination toward women exists. They are often the mothers and wives and sisters of the entrenched who are denied their rightful inheritance to fulfill their potential. By denying marginal people the opportunity to pursue their unique perspectives to the conclusion of their products, we deny society an opportunity to evolve and change.

THE EFFECTS OF ACTUALIZERS

The actualizers' high levels of functioning can be established. They tend to function with intensity and stamina physically; with a sense of external mission beyond their personal fulfillment emotivationally; very initiatively interpersonally; by breaking their substantive specialties out at the level of detailed steps that others can use; by developing their own individualized action programs; and by helping others to develop their own individualized learning programs. Perhaps what cannot be measured easily are their marginal perspectives, the effects of these perspectives upon their unique products, and the effects of these products upon the variability of the system within which they exist.

Let us take two views of society—the first of a system that is not free; and the second of a free system. We will represent each initially as a normal curve and then follow the course of their process (Berenson, 1978). As can be seen, in any normally distributed population, the masses are mainstreamed in the middle of the curve (see Figure 10-1). The further we range from the central tendencies the fewer people there are and the more marginal are the people. Depending upon what human dimensions we are measuring, the people at the extremes will be high or low in their functioning.

To the great horde of people massing in or near the center, the people at either extreme may look the same. And, indeed, depending upon how the marginal peoples manage the crises they encounter, they may be made to be the same. Thus, for example, Black infants selected at random in rural Mississippi yield a developmental I.Q. of 117, approaching the superior range and reflecting a superior nervous system, which is the basis for intelligence. They are on the high margin of intelligence when compared to a mean I.Q. of 100. Yet with the inability of their protectors—their parents and others—to

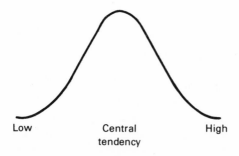

Figure 10-1   The variability in society

facilitate the development of their intelligence, by the time they are school age they are already marginally low in intelligence, functioning in the 80 I.Q. range, which is borderline defective. Depending upon the school experiences they receive, they may go even further out on the low end of the continuum (Carkhuff and Berenson, 1976).

Perhaps the most basic issue to address is whether we can reverse this tendency. For example, can we not only maintain the initially high level of functioning of children with superior nervous systems but can we also cause initially low level children to function at high levels? The answer is "Yes!" Research was conducted by Rick Heber and his associates in Milwaukee, Wisconsin. Taking the infants of borderline defective mothers (80 I.Q. range), they had helpers teach the mothers how to stimulate and respond to the children. At school age, the children of the mothers in the experimental group had I.Q.'s 25 to 30 points greater than the children in the control group, who had the predicted 80 I.Q.'s that are resultant from being left alone to be reared as they would ordinarily be reared (Bronfenbrenner, 1974; Heber, et al., 1971; Skeels, 1966; Skodak and Skeels, 1949).

The stories of Mississippi and Milwaukee are the stories of two societies—one bound in the chains of nonresponsive institutionalization; the other free and facilitative of human development. It makes no difference what style the institutionalized society has—whether apparently free and democratic or totalitarian and enslaved. If it does not facilitate the variability of its members, it institutionalizes the demands upon their development. What matters is the substance of the society; that is, whether it not only freely allows for but also facilitates the variability of its members.

The destruct system

The central tendency in an unfree society becomes institutionalized (see Figure 10-2). The first stage may be conceived of as an ignorance stage, and ignorance is always intentional. As can be seen, the logical goal of facilitating peoples' development toward a higher level of functioning is ignored. This situation occurs when those in the mainstream treat high functioning people just as they treat low functioning people. It is just too much work for the comfortable people to become productive people. At most they need energy only to adapt to their circumstances; they are caught up in an incentive system that demands very little and rewards them handsomely; they care not about the people around them; they get away with vague concepts of efforts at work; they involve themselves only in the minimum learning necessary to insure their comfort; they are concerned only with being critics, diagnosing others from an external frame of reference. They seek to institutionalize these characteristics and make people over in their images. That way they will always be comfortable and never be vulnerable—even as they die, physically, emotionally, and intellectually.

What happens during the second stage of the Destruct System, a stage of restriction, is that the variability becomes more and more restricted. This is accomplished by channeling the extremes on any index into the mainstream. Thus, the highs and the lows become fewer and less prominent and the central tendency is accentuated.

This restrictiveness is carried to an extreme of leptokurticism during the third stage of elimination. During this stage those marginal peoples—high and low—who were not mainstreamed for one reason or another are eliminated. Thus, the central tendency is further exaggerated as the peoples come increasingly to look like each other.

The fourth stage may be conceived of as a destructive phase, although the process has been destructive throughout. Finally, all variance is destroyed and encompassed within one dimension on any one index. We see this most clearly in advanced stages of all authoritarian societies. The people are made over in the image of their leader or leaders.

The fifth stage of institutionalization may be considered the disappearing stage. Since all peoples appear as one, they can be represented as one. Indeed, the one can be reduced until it has disappeared. The culmination of the institutionalization of humanity is the disappearance of humanity. We see this most clearly in the advanced stages of all totalitarian societies. The people are made over

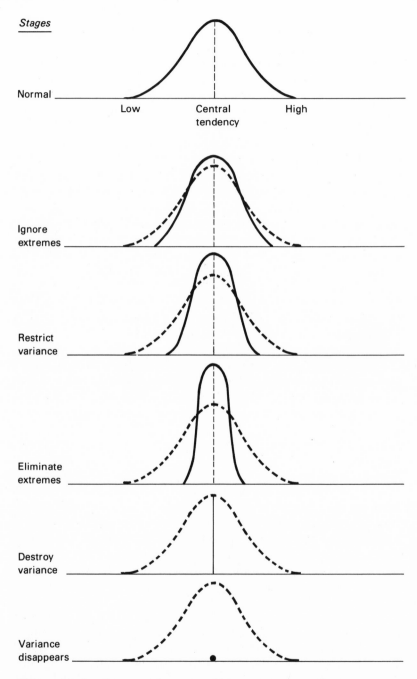

Figure 10-2 The movement toward restricted variability of unfree societies

in the image of their leader or leaders. And their leaders are one-dimensional people with one principle of operating—either you are controlled or you are eliminated. In the end, such a system self-destructs.

Even when such a system is overthrown, as in a revolution from within or without, the stages are usually repeated: One source of restrictive variance is replaced with another. Surely, there is utility in doing this when a system is diseased. However, such a program kills or cures. It does not grow because it maximizes intervention and control and abandons or dislocates or eliminates sources of variance.

The construct system

The central tendency in a free society becomes mobilized (see Figure 10–3). The first stage may be conceived of as a focusing stage. In a sense, the main body of the variance targets the marginal person. It observes the success of the marginal person's operations. And if a significant number of its people—perhaps ten to twenty percent—are attracted to it, it mobilizes to incorporate it.

During the second stage of the Construct System, the main body of variance begins to approach the successful marginal person. The curve begins to be skewed in the direction of the marginal person as the society seeks to incorporate his or her healthful potency.

In the third stage, the society incorporates the successful marginal person. In the process of being skewed fully in the direction of the marginal person, there is a tendency for the tail in the other, less functional direction to diminish in size. Thus, people at the less functional end of the continuum are mobilized to move toward the main body of variance.

In the fourth stage, the society embodies the successful marginal person. In a sense, it has mainstreamed the successful attributes and made them the mode rather than the deviation. At the same time, it is eliminating more of the variance from the less functional end of the continuum.

Finally, in the last stage, the society actually enhances the attributes of the successful marginal person. It models and, thus, represents what was once deviant. Also, whether inadvertently or not, it sets the stage for the new variations off the now main-streamed theme. Thus, by representing the attributes of the once marginal person, society creates the conditions for the development

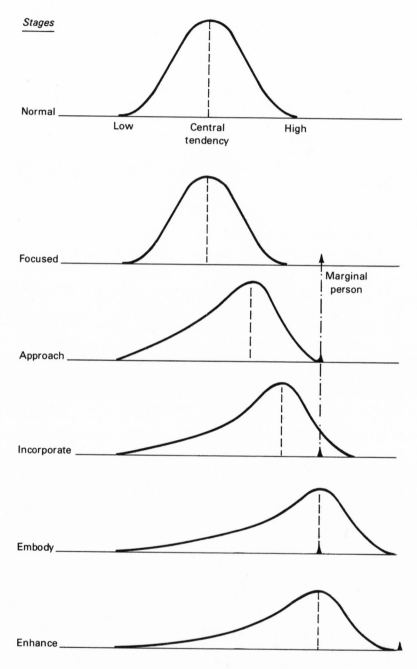

Figure 10-3 The movement toward increasing variability in free societies

of newly marginal people who will serve to move society still further in the direction of effectiveness.

In summary, the Construct System produces a people who are more variable in a relative sense and more healthy in an absolute sense. A society dominated by such a system is always skewed in the direction of the fully functioning. Such a society is always creating variability by its tolerance limits and its evolutionary response disposition. Such a society is always moving toward effectiveness and, thus, toward health.

Such a Construct System is an evolutionary system. Rather than to replace our restricted source of variance with another as in a revolutionary system, it adds variance incrementally. It works effectively when there are healthy aspects of the system to be incorporated and these healthy aspects, in turn, evolve in a free society. It grows by minimizing intervention or control and maximizing variance. It maximizes existing sources of variance by adding incrementally without fundamental alterations.

In the beginning, people are in trouble because they have too few responses available to them. Along the way, fewer people are in difficulty because more people have a larger repertoire of responses. In the end, such a system has extensive variability among people functioning at high levels of whatever index is employed.

Such a system is consistent with the laws of science and nature. It is organic in terms of utilizing its own resources as the source of its own power. It is dynamic in terms of evolving constantly in more and more efficacious forms. It conserves energy in minimizing its investment and maximizing its return. It allows evolution to work at a maximum rate in maximizing the contribution of humans to humans.

The key to the development of a relatively more variable and absolutely more healthy society is the variability of the fully functioning person. The fully functioning person is, by definition, more variable on certain specialty dimensions than the society in which he or she exists. (Indeed, the fully functioning person is infinitely more variable than all other totalitarian societies summed together on that person's specialty dimensions.) It is precisely this variability that makes it attractive for society to move toward the fully functioning person to incorporate him or her. It is also this same variability that distinguishes the fully functioning person from other marginal peoples who are dysfunctional but with whom totalitarian societies tend to confuse the fully functioning person.

In turn, the key to the fully functioning person's variability is his or her marginality—the ability to see things from a unique perspective; to see the subtle nuances of old dimensions; to develop the full richness of new dimensions. It is this marginality coupled with the development of one's physical, emotional, and intellectual resources that enable the fully functioning person to actualize his or her human potential and to give society the opportunity to actualize its potential.

In conclusion, the healthy society is moving in the direction of the actualizers—the once marginal people other societies sought to eliminate. Actualizers are the sources of creativity and productivity constructive societies seek to cultivate. Such a society is seeking to emulate the vision of Milwaukee—to make it probable that little kids become free and productive adults. Such a society is moving in the direction of its own self-actualization. Such a society is within our grasp.

REFERENCES

Berenson, B. G. *Human Values and Human Technology.* Keynote Address, Belo Horizonte, Brazil, April, 1978.

Bronfenbrenner, U. *A Report on Longitudinal Evaluations of Preschool Programs. Vol. II. Is Early Intervention Effective?* Washington, D.C.: HEW, 1974.

Carkhuff, R. R. and Berenson, B. G. *Teaching as Treatment.* Amherst, Mass.: Human Resource Development Press, 1976.

Heber, R.; Garber, H.; Harington, S.; and Hoffman, C. *Rehabilitation of Families at Risk for Mental Retardation.* Madison, Wisc.: Rehabilitation Research and Training Center in Mental Retardation, University of Wisconsin, 1972.

Skeels, H. M. *Adult Status of Children from Contrasting Early Life Experiences.* Monographs of the Society for Research in Child Development, 1966, *31,* Serial #105.

Skodak, M. and Skeels, H. M. A Final Follow-Up Study of 100 Adopted Children. *Journal of Genetic Psychology,* 1949, *75,* 85–125.

VI
Models of actualizing

11

A model for actualizing human potential

I looked into the eyes of the secondary students in a Brazilian school. I experienced the bright glow of their inner strength. I felt the vitality of raw energy. I heard the spontaneity of their "fradimo" humor, where they devilishly play tricks on their authoritarian mentors. I tasted the love of their open faces. And I responded empathically to what I saw.

"I am excited to find you so happy," I was interpreted to them. "School has not yet worn you down."

They laughed fully with their bodies and their heads. "Besides education," one boy boldly asked, "what else can take the life out of us?"

"Only you, yourselves!" I answered, "Because you have not yet been taught to be winners. As losers, you are doomed to take one step forward and two steps back."

"How can we learn to become winners?" another followed thoughtfully.

"You already have the essential physical ingredient—your vitality. Your energy is intact and fully available to you."

They nodded affirmatively.

"You also, obviously, have your emotional ingredients working for you. You are open and spontaneous."

They waited expectantly.

"And you are inquisitive. What you lack, however, are the essential intellectual ingredients—the skills to produce creative products. Like your land, you are a raw material that has not yet been tapped."

"When you have the skills, then you must develop the discipline to commit them with diligence to growth—yours as well as the people around you."

"What will we have when we have the skills and the discipline?" a young girl asked.

"You will have the ability to help to shape your own personal destiny and to help your country to shape its destiny."

They attended me with intensity.

"Then Brazil will have the destiny which is yours."

With a great surge forward, they stood spontaneously and applauded.

I was deeply touched by their enthusiastic reception and moved by their resolve to follow my charge to them. They were motivated by a sense of destiny. They had an experience of something important within them. They felt impelled to give birth to this experience. But they did not know its shape or functions.

HUMAN POTENTIAL

To be sure, a sense of destiny and a sense of actualizing human potential are inextricably bound. What is human potential if not a sense of personal destiny? What is destiny if not the process of actualizing human potential? Both terms reflect pictures of what can be. Given the resources, given the skills, given the discipline and, above all, given the work, both are limited only by the imagination of the people who conceive them.

In this context, perhaps we can take a moment and think about what is meant by actualizing human potential. What is human potential? How do we actualize it?

Some of us perhaps cannot conceive of actualizing human potential. Many will think of the process of becoming "free" and "spontaneous." Most will think in terms of "independence" and "autonomy." Some few will conceive of being able to "help themselves and others."

Depending upon the maturity of their formulators, these definitions will communicate different meanings. To some, being free means being able to decide what we want to do each day. To others, it means the ability to engage in new learning experiences.

For some people, being independent means "not needing anyone." For others, it means "being able to guide the direction of one's own life."

For some people, helping means "performing certain roles in life." For others, it means "helping oneself first before helping others."

I will share my definition of actualizing human potential: *developing human resources*. Although this appears to be a simple definition, its implications are profound.

Developing human resources means developing our own as well as others. We cannot develop our resources fully if we are not also involved in developing those of others. Developing human resources is a simultaneous and reciprocal process between the helper and the person being helped.

Such a definition of human potential means that we are in the process of helping or being helped in all life situations. Indeed, it is impossible to help without simultaneously being helped. It is impossible to help another without first entering that person's phenomenological frame of reference, and thus, having the dimensions of our own humanity expanded.

We grow with this expansion of our human dimensions. In so doing, we are helped in the process of helping. Our resources are developed in the process of developing those of others.

At the highest levels of developing human resources, we are teaching and learning. We are teaching to others the dimensions we have developed. We are learning from others the dimensions we have not developed. We are constantly expanding our human dimensions. This expansion of human dimensions is the essence of actualizing human potential.

What, then, are these dimensions of human potential? What is their structure?

The structure of human potential

When we think of the dimensions of human potential we most often think of the affective or emotional and the cognitive or intellectual dimensions. Such thinking is appropriate, for these are the dimensions that make us most uniquely human. But just as the intellectual has its foundation in the emotional so are both supported by the physical dimension.

The structure of human potential, then, must be considered to include *physical, emotional,* and *intellectual* resource dimensions (see Figure 11-1). Thus, for example, persons actualizing their physical potential will be functioning physically with high levels of intensity and stamina. Their level of physical fitness in terms of cardiorespiratory, endurance, strength, and flexibility will provide them with the energy they require to function effectively in any area of endeavor. The base of life remains physical, and they use this base to support the other human dimensions.

Persons actualizing their emotional potential will be functioning emotionally with high levels of responsiveness and initiative. Both in relation to themselves and others, they will be able to respond to human experience and to initiate courses of action based upon the understanding of that human experience. An essential component of human experience remains emotional, the subjective experience of objective reality.

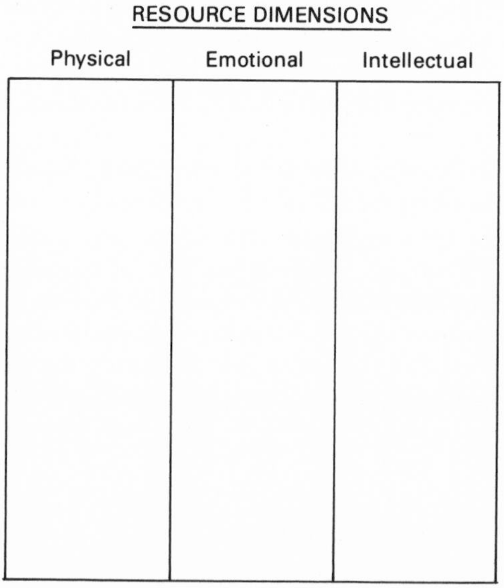

RESOURCE DIMENSIONS

Physical	Emotional	Intellectual

Figure 11-1   The structure of human potential

Persons actualizing their intellectual potential will be functioning intellectually with high levels of skills and supportive knowledge. They will be able to organize the facts and concepts of their daily experiences into principles and to translate those principles into skill objectives and skill steps. They will be guided more and more by their intellectual development, which does after all distinguish us most from all other forms of life.

Human resources are actualized when they are translated into skill applications. Skills are observable and measurable, replicable and teachable, and, therefore, achievable. We can determine the degree to which people have actualized their human potential by the quantity and quality of skills they have. In a growing person these skills are constantly expanding in quantity and elevating in quality.

In short, skills offer us the way to see and demonstrate our human potential. Skills are the operational representations of the dimensions of human potential. The process of skills development constitutes the equation for actualizing human potential:

Skills development = Actualizing human potential

The application of developed or acquired skills comprises the equation for actualized human potential:

Skills application = Actualized human potential

Thus, physical dimensions may be actualized in fitness skills development and application. Emotional dimensions may be actualized in interpersonal skills development and application. Intellectual dimensions may be actualized in conceptual skills development and application.

What, then, are these applications of human potential? What are the functions of human potential?

The functions of human potential

When we think of the applications of actualized human potential, we think of the areas of daily life situations we encounter. We think of living situations in the home and community; learning situations at school; working situations on the job. In short, we think of *living, learning,* and *working* skills applications (see Figure 11–2).

Persons with high levels of resource development demonstrate their actualization in living, learning, and working applications. Thus, they may apply their physical fitness skills in application in the living, learning, and working areas. For example, they may live

STRUCTURE:
RESOURCE DIMENSIONS

Functions:	Physical	Emotional	Intellectual
Skill Applications			
Living			
Learning			
Working			

Figure 11-2 The structure and functions of human potential

at a level of personal hygiene that allows them to grow free of disease and its accompanying dissipation of energies. Such cleanliness is truly next to godliness because it enables them to more closely approach the limits of their human potential uncontaminated by debilitating human experiences.

Actualized persons may apply their emotional-interpersonal skills in problem-solving applications in the living, learning, and working areas. Thus, for example, in the learning area, they may help themselves and others to make effective decisions in learning. They can use their interpersonal skills to elicit input; to define problems and goals; to expand alternative courses of action; to operationalize and prioritize values and choose preferred courses of action. Such emotional skill applications constitute the core interpersonal learning experience.

Actualized persons may also apply intellectual skills in living, learning, and working applications. Thus, for example, in the working area, they may use their concept development skills to make career applications. They can use their concept development skills to expand career alternatives; narrow career alternatives in terms of personal values and occupational requirements; develop planning, placement, promotion, and productivity programs. Such intellectual skill applications constitute the core of career development.

Thus, the structural dimensions of human potential interact with the functional applications. Together, the dimensions and applications allow us to define the goal of human potential. It remains for us to define the process by which we actualize human potential.

THE ACTUALIZATION PROCESS

The process by which human potential is actualized is learning. Learning involves the acquisition of new responses. It is characterized by an *exploration* of the learning experience; an *understanding* of the learning goals; and an *action* program to acquire the learning (see Figure 11–3). These phases of learning constitute the process for developing human resources.

Thus, in exploring the learning experience, the learners will analyze the learning tasks and diagnose their own abilities in terms of the tasks. For example, in relation to physical fitness skills applied in the living area, the learners may analyze the skill and knowledge requirements of the personal hygiene tasks and diagnose themselves in terms of their abilities to perform the skills and knowledge. This learning exploration will enable them to know where they are in relation to the learning experience.

In understanding the learning goals, the learners will set learning objectives in relation to their levels of skills and knowledge diagnosed in the exploration. For example, in relation to interpersonal skills as applied in the learning area, the learners may develop problem-solving objectives based upon the diagnosis of their skills and knowledge. Such learning objectives will enable them to know where they are in relation to where they want or need to be with the learning objectives.

In acting to achieve the learning goals, the learners will implement step-by-step learning programs calculated to develop the skills and knowledge required to achieve the learning goals. For example, in relation to the concept development skills applied in the working area, the learners may learn the skills steps and the supportive facts, concepts, and principles required to master career development skills. Such learning programs will enable the learners to act to get from where they are to where they want to be in the working area.

The goal of human potential, then, is defined by its structure and functions. The actualization of human potential is defined by

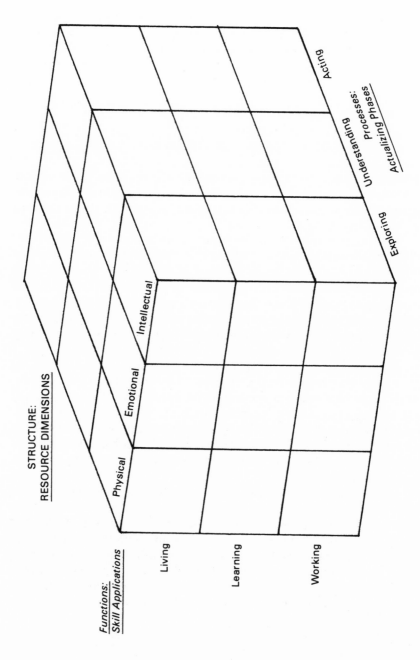

STRUCTURE:
RESOURCE DIMENSIONS

Physical   Emotional   Intellectual

Functions:
Skill Applications

Living

Learning

Working

Exploring   Understanding   Acting
processes:
Actualizing Phases

Figure 11-3 The structure, function, and actualization process of human potential

the learning process required to achieve its structure and functions. Input is processed through the cycles of learning and output involves skill products. The learners are cycled through the phases of learning in successive approximations of the physical, emotional, and intellectual skills required to make living, learning, and working applications. These successive approximations of actualization constitute the developmental stages of actualization.

The actualization stages

The developmental stages of actualization are characterized by movement toward and beyond independence (see Figure 11–4). From an unactualized stage of *dependency* upon others for learning, learners move in successive approximations toward becoming their own teachers. Actualizers strive for *independence* in areas where they can process their own input and produce their own output and *interdependency* in areas where they can teach themselves and others the content they want or need to know while learning from others at the same time.

Initially, learners are dependent upon others for their learning. Consequently, they usually have only partial or incomplete learning. Some have only the experience of exploration. Some have only the shared insights of others. Some become implementers of the action programs of others. Many have no real learning at all. They do not own their learning experiences. They are ineffective learners.

As learners move toward independency, they maintain their own learning processes—receiving stimuli, exploring their dimensions, understanding their goals, acting upon their programs. They do not require others to help them although they can use effective helping experiences. The learners own their learning experiences. They are effective learners.

At the stage of independency, learners become dependent upon themselves for efficient and effective learning. They now have the helping skills to facilitate their own learning as well as that of others, the attentive skills to receive stimuli, the responsive skills to extract the subjective feeling and objective reality, the personalization skills to define personal problems and goals, the initiative skills to develop action programs to achieve personal goals. The learners become, in effect, their own self-helpers as well as helpers of others.

Finally, at the highest levels, learners achieve the state of interdependency. At this stage, they have the skills to teach themselves

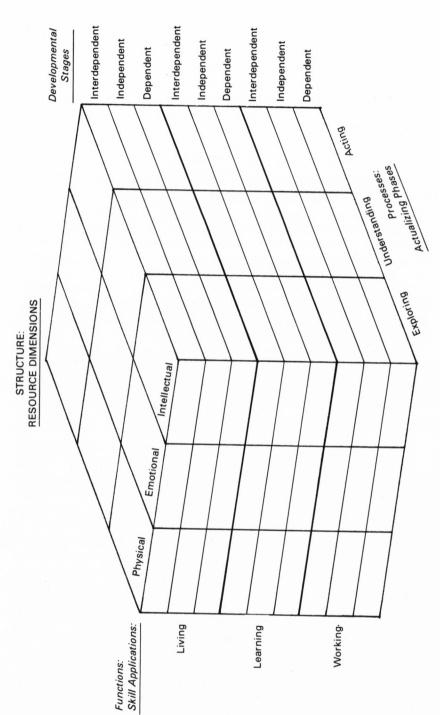

Figure 11-4 Model for actualizing human potential

and others the content they want or need to learn. At these levels they are developing content to skills objectives, diagnosing learners in terms of their skills levels, setting learning goals based upon the skills diagnosis, delivering the learning steps to achieve the skills content. The learners become, in effect, self-teachers. As well, they teach others and learn from them the content others can teach most efficiently and effectively.

Thus, the developmental stages of actualization interact with the phases of learning. The learner moves from other-learning dependency through self-learning independency to self- and other-teaching interdependency.

SUMMARY

The structure of human potential is defined by the dimensions of human resources—physical, emotional, and intellectual dimensions. The functions of human potential are defined by the applications of skills in different areas of life situations—living, learning, and working applications.

The actualization process is operationalized by the learning required to acquire the structure and functions of human potential—exploring, understanding, and acting. The developmental stages are characterized by successive approximations of actualizing human potential—dependency, independency, inner-dependency, and inter-dependency.

The structure of human potential, then, is defined by the resource dimensions and the functions by the skill applications. Succinctly, the structure and functions of human potential express size or variability (or quantity and quality of responses).

The actualization process is operationalized by the recycling of learning through the developmental stages. The function of the actualization process is to grow in size and variability (or quantity and quality of responses).

Now, let us reformulate a more operational definition of actualizing human potential: *the learning process for increasing the quantity and quality of our physical, emotional, and intellectual responses for living, learning, and working applications.* In other words, actualizing human potential is the process of becoming a fully functioning human being.

It is just such a human potential goal that the Brazilian students shared with enthusiasm in their views of destiny, their own and that of their country. Secure in the knowledge that we are either growing or dying—actualizing or denying our potential, we are forever standing on the tips of our toes, stretching our bodies, souls, and minds to reach with the tips of our fingers. We are in the process of becoming our destiny.

People who have a destiny are people who have a dream.

People who actualize their human potential are people who live a dream.

After my experience with the Brazilian school children, while I was moving between classes, one of the educators offered an apology for their behavior:

"They are so young. They still think that they can change the world."

My song is dedicated to those people, young in mind and soul, pregnant with their own destinies, who believe that they can change things:

I am change

If they are young who think
That they can change the world,
I am a newborn infant—
I am change unfurled.

You can chalk me on the blackboards
Or scratch me in the sand.
You can shout me in the chorus
That builds throughout the land.

Chorus: *You can see me in the eyes of children*
And hear me in their song.
You can taste my sweet breath in the wind
And feel me being born.

You can find me in the skills you learn—
You can use my eyes to see.
For when they teach you what is known,
You'll discover what can be.

You can join me in the nation's womb
As we fashion our freedom.
For I am change and change alone
Can forge a human being.

Chorus: *You can see me in the eyes of children*
And hear me in their song.
You can taste my sweet breath in the wind
And feel me being born.

12
The process of actualizing human potential

The newborn infant enters the world with little with which to relate other than physiological reflex responses. Thus, for example, the child has the sucking reflex and the palmar or grasping reflex. One of the ways we guide our children is by helping them to form habits. Habits may be acquired by associating or relating, in space and time, two or more sets of activities. At least one of these activities must satisfy some human need for the human behavior to be repeated as a habit. For example, the child may develop the sucking habit when nourished by the mother's breast. The results may be said to be instrumental in satisfying the child's need for nourishment.

Human learning and, indeed, human intelligence, begins to manifest itself when the child is several months old. At this point, the children begin to explore themselves and their environments. The children become aware of the association of the stimuli to which they have become conditioned and the responses that have been conditioned to the stimuli. They become aware of causes and effects in their worlds. This awareness is a two-way street. For example, the child becomes aware that the nipple or the food serves as stimulus to a sucking or grasping response. This response, in turn, will lead to satisfying a need for nourishment. The child may also become aware that a need for nourishment stimulates the response of search for the nipple or the food.

It is a short step from becoming aware of the ingredients of human experience to anticipating experiences. With the increasing confidence in this awareness of the relationship of stimulus and responses, the child is prepared for purposeful learning at about one year of age. In other words, the child sets out to obtain a certain result or end, independent of the means to be employed. For example, the child may set out to attract mother or obtain food or an object that is out of reach. Drawing from this awareness of cause and effect, the child sets a goal of achieving certain effects. The goals of the purposeful act often are seen only later, although some approximation of them was obviously intended from the beginning.

The next phase of human learning flows naturally from the understanding phase. It involves the development of behavior patterns instrumental to achieving goals. From the end of the first year on the child draws from his or her repertoire of behaviors to produce the responses needed to achieve the goal. For example, the child may laugh or cry to bring the mother. The child may move a hand in the direction of the unreachable food or object. There may be a series of trial-and-error experiences. These experiences may confirm the child's responses through reaching the goal and experiencing satisfaction or rejecting the child's responses through not reaching the goal.

The first year of human development serves as a prototype for all human learning. The child's reflexes are unknowingly conditioned as habitual responses to certain stimuli. These habits serve as the limited repertoire of responses with which the child initially approaches the world. Improvement in the quantity and quality of responses with which the adult ultimately relates to the world depends upon the development of the child's intelligence. This, in turn, depends upon how effectively he or she learns.

Initially, the child explores and identifies the nature of the stimuli and responses in his or her experience. Transitionally, the child comes to understand the interactive nature of stimuli and responses, anticipating the effects of one upon the other and developing goals to achieve these effects. Finally, the child acts

*by drawing from his or her developing repertoire of responses to
attempt to achieve the goals. The child's action behavior is
shaped by the feedback or the effects he or she achieves in the
environment. This feedback recycles the stages or phases of
learning as the child explores more extensively, understands
more accurately, and acts more effectively. This ascending,
enlarging spiral of exploration, understanding, and action is the
source of the adults' improving repertoire of responses.*

*What goes on in the first year of life goes on in more and
more refined ways throughout life—or not. How effectively we
live our lives depends totally upon how efficiently and effectively
we learn.*

Perhaps the dominant characteristic of the fully functioning person
is his or her disposition to learning. For the fully functioning person,
learning is growth and growth is life. The whole person makes a
choice to be a full participant in life. In so doing, he or she involves
those around in either full participation in their lives or rejection of
full participation as a way of life. The fully functioning person can
be joined in a very intense relationship—or that intensity can be
rejected. But, he or she cannot be ignored.

LEARNING PROCESSES

Life is found in subjective experience and objective reality. The process by which we receive, process, and produce subjective experience
and objective reality is learning (see Figure 12-1). The learning process may be organized in a systematic way, just the way the human
system operates when it is functioning most fully to learn from
human experience.

The necessary beginning function involves the receptiveness
of the human system to receiving the experiential and informational
input. The system must be open to and, indeed, facilitative of all
stimuli impinging upon it. It must be vigilant in attentively opening
its receptors to all human experience.

All effective systems receive inputs.

What the human system of the fully functioning person does with
the input comes next. The effective system analyzes the input, diagnoses its needs in relation to the analysis, personalizes its goals, and
individualizes its action programs to achieve the goals.

All effective systems process data.

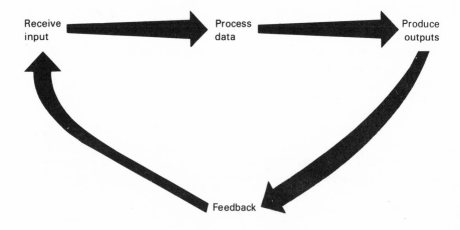

Figure 12-1   Growth is a learning system

It follows naturally that the effective human system acts upon or implements the action program. In other words, it integrates the experiential and informational data to produce meaningful products.

All effective systems produce outputs.

The effective system continues by receiving feedback from the outputs. That is to say, the effective system receives the feedback from the impact of its focused delivery. It learns the degree to which the delivery was effective. This feedback serves as new input to stimulate the learning system once again.

All effective systems are shaped by feedback.

It may seem paradoxical that a system that is initially open to input becomes focused in its output. Yet, this is the only way a system can expand—by first expanding with input and then narrowing toward output.

THE LEARNING SYSTEM

There are certain dimensions that fully functioning people moving toward actualization have. These dimensions make the learning process full and fluid and effective. These dimensions characterize fully functioning people during the inputting, processing, and outputting phases of the learning process (see Figure 12-2).

Input

First and foremost among these characteristics is high physical energy. A high energy level enables people to maintain a high level of vigilance and attentiveness to incoming stimuli or input. This high level of attentiveness does not mean that the person is constantly mobilized. Rather, it is characteristic of fully functioning people to operate at very low levels of energy output. For example, their pulse rates are typically low. However, they mobilize immediately when the stimuli occur. Further, fully functioning people have made fine discriminations concerning incoming stimuli. In other words, they know what they are looking for. It is as if they have an internal gyroscope that lets them know when they should be attentive. They use the input to which they have attended to initiate their processing of the stimuli.

Processing

The attentiveness to the incoming experiential and informational stimuli sets the processing mechanism of fully functioning people into operation. In the first phase of processing, fully functioning people evidence a high tolerance for the exploration of the input. They delay further processing until they have used all of their senses to explore all of the input. This tolerance is psychological in nature and is translated in responsiveness to the stimuli. Fully functioning people suspect their judgments concerning the experience and respond accurately to their experience of the stimuli. Thus, they respond interchangeably to both the experiential and informational meaning of the stimuli for them. In other words, they respond to the feeling the stimuli evokes and the reason for the feeling. All of this occurs while the people are actively analyzing the stimuli into their component parts, processes, and functions and diagnosing themselves with regard to their ability to function with those parts, processes, and functions. For example, people may analyze the stimuli and diagnose themselves in terms of the skills and knowledge required for functioning in a particular area. The products of this responsiveness to the stimuli, then, are individualized needs assessments of where the people are in relation to the stimuli.

In the second phase of processing, fully functioning people integrate the experiential and informational dimensions of the stimuli. They integrate the subjective experience and objective

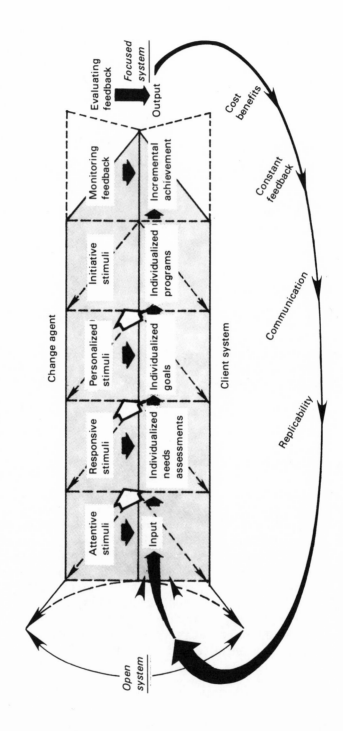

Figure 12-2 The learning system

reality in a wholistic response. They attempt to understand where they are or need to be in the learning experience. Fully functioning people integrate their experience by relating the wholistic response to their personalized frame of reference. They do so by internalizing responsibility for overcoming personal obstacles and achieving personal goals. For example, they may personalize the feeling and meaning of their experience by understanding their role in its evolution. They may personalize the problems and goals from their response deficits. The products of this personalized understanding of the stimuli are individualized goals.

During the third phase of processing, the responsive and personalized stimuli set the initiative stimuli into operation. During the personalizing phase, the focus was narrowed in individualized goals. Now the focus will be further narrowed by operationalizing the goals and technologizing the means to achieve them. Operationalizing involves breaking the goals down into the operations that comprise them. Technologizing means developing the systems and technologies needed to achieve them. The products of initiating with the stimuli, then, are the individualized programs developed to achieve individualized goals.

Thus, fully functioning people have transformed an initially open system into a sharply focused product. It remains for them to follow-up by monitoring the feedback from the implementation of the individualized programs. With the implementation of each step of the program, the people must ask and answer questions concerning the correctness of their implementation: "Am I doing this step correctly?" Modifications will be made in the program steps based upon this feedback. The product of monitoring feedback is the incremental movement toward the achievement of the goal.

Output

The last remaining function of the fully functioning learning system is to evaluate the feedback from the application or use of the product. That is, the evaluative feedback answers the question: "How did the product or output impact the audience or environment for which it was intended?" The feedback process involves a full evaluation of the costs as well as the benefits for the target populations: "Was it worth the effort and expense?" The evaluative feedback is recycled into the processing system as new input—to be diagnosed in individualized needs assessments for its current effects, to set new individualized goals for more desirable effects, to develop new individualized programs to achieve the goals. Thus, fully functioning people develop what may be considered constant feedback systems. These systems enable them to move by successive approximations of effectiveness in shaping new products. Fueled by the constant feedback, fully functioning people use their processing skills not only to produce more effective products but also more replicable products. In a very real sense, the constant feedback system serves to generate its own learning in a never-ending succession of approximations of meaningful and effective human products.

LEARNING BY-PRODUCTS

There are a number of by-products of the learning system of fully functioning people or actualizers. These serve to characterize their functioning in terms that are more familiar to most people. Yet, these characteristics flow directly from the learning system underlying them.

In this context, perhaps the dominant characteristic of fully functioning or actualized people is their autonomy: *Actualizers realize that they must be their own pathfinders and travel roads never traveled before.*

Equipped only with learning or growing skills, actualizers develop their own directions, recognizing full well that every step offers less and less guidance and more and more growth.

In this regard, the actualizers' stances toward input can be described best by their attitude toward the stimuli of life: *Actualizers view input as the source of life.*

They view the incoming stimuli as the source of constant new learning. As such they welcome the input with a sense of intense excitement. Their openness is their receiving mechanism for life. Input is a precondition of learning, and thus, life.

With regard to processing, actualizers recognize the inadequacy of receiving input. Indeed, they recognize the central significance of the role of systematic exploration and understanding in the development of new insights into the input: *Actualizers systematically develop insights into life's inputs.*

The key word here is systematic because they realize that insights that do not evolve developmentally are useless. They are useless because each piece does not build upon the previous input, because they cannot be replicated in new learning situations, and because they do not foster action.

With regard to output, then, actualizers recognize that insight without action is impotent. Just as they systematically develop their insights so do they systematically develop the action programs that flow from the insights: *Actualizers systematically develop action programs from their insights.*

Actualizers recognize that life is empty without acting. A life without acting is a life without risk. And in a life without risk, no one wins, no one learns, and everyone loses. Thus, whatever they do, they do fully in an integrated output of energy. Creativity and productivity become a way of life for actualizers, as they realize that life can be found in initiative behavior.

Again, learning can be found in the recycling stimulated by the feedback from the initiative output. Once people have acted, they receive feedback, which recycles the learning process: *Actualizers learn from the systematic processing of the feedback from the output.*

Actualizers realize that life is a continuous learning process. The full life requires discriminations concerning the effectiveness of the products of learning and an evaluation of the investments required to achieve that level of effectiveness. In other words, actualizers are constantly engaged in a cost-benefit analysis of life that sharpens values and priorities and refines products and efficiencies.

In summary, actualizers are aware of the awesome responsibilities that come with freedom. They must do more than know all there is to know about their life and work to stay whole and to extend their boundaries. They must go beyond the known to meet their responsibilities to their own integrity, knowing that without this, they cannot act responsibly with and for another person: *The actualizers recognize that the vehicle to freedom and for responsibilities is learning.*

In the end, actualizers value truth above all else. Honesty becomes a way of life as fully functioning people recognize that they can be only as creative as they are honest.

VII
Summary and conclusions

13
$$E = P \cdot E^2 \cdot I^3$$

There is a story told by Venezuelans about themselves. When God made the Earth, He provided differentially according to His purposes. In some areas He provided great oceans and rivers for fishing, in others forests for hunting, or grasslands and croplands for farming, or raw materials for mining. In Venezuela, He provided everything—mighty oceans and deep rivers, rain forests and abundant farmlands, oil and gas and coal, and gold and silver and raw materials of all kinds. Then someone said to God that it was unlike Him to give so much to one land. And God answered: "Yes, but now I am going to put people there."

The story of actualizing human potential is similar. The opportunities are rich; the potential unlimited. The only disadvantage is people. It is the people alone who limit human potential.

There are many models for human development (Chapter 2). All fall shy of inclusive and operational definition. What they do offer are some dimensions that can be incorporated and integrated in definitions of the fully functioning person.

Historically, Maslow went the furthest in terms of developing some principles of self-actualization (Chapter 3). He postulated many dimensions of actualization—cultural, philosophical, emotional, interpersonal, and intellectual. While his thinking was comprehensive in terms of the emotional and interpersonal dimensions, he did not think cumulatively in terms of incorporating physical dimensions. In addition, he did not emphasize the intellectual dimensions as the most potent in terms of actualizing human potential. Finally, while he gave us principles, he did not contribute to operationalizing and, thus, making these dimensions achievable. In the words of Aspy, "He gave us a glimpse of heaven without giving us any way to get there."

Perhaps the most difficult task is to postulate the dimensions of human potential (Chapter 4). When we studied self-actualizing people, we found the following dimensions to be critical—physical fitness and the physical energy flow that is resultant from it, emotional commitments to a mission outside oneself, interpersonal relations that lead to incorporating the missions of others, substantive specialty skills leading to skilled expertise, learning skills leading to the processing of data, teaching skills leading to the communication of content. The bottom line is that actualizers are skilled people while non-actualizers are unskilled people.

The most important source of actualizing human potential is the ability to develop insights systematically and to develop the action programs flowing from these insights systematically (Chapter 5). Helpers serve to facilitate development of insights and action by the following additional sources: modeling and imitation, expectancies or expectations, participation and motivation, and reinforcement or rewards. In the end, the actualization of human potential is found in carrying the responsive and initiative dimensions out in a spiraling movement toward life.

The measurement of human potential is yet another skill (Chapter 6). We must be able to operationalize the dimensions of human potential to achieve them. Thus, we found that actualizers were functioning with the following levels of the dimensions: physical stamina, emotivational missions, interpersonal initiative, intellectual skill steps, learning skills, and teaching skills. The levels of functioning of those operating at less than full levels flowed from these definitions. The physical dimensions served to energize; the emotional dimensions served as catalysts to motivate; the intellectual dimensions served to actualize human potential.

The data comparing actualizers and non-actualizers are consistent. While actualizers are relatively highest intellectually, non-actualizers are relatively lowest intellectually (Chapter 7). In other words, the real distinguishing characteristic between actualizers and non-actualizers is to be found in their intellectual functioning. Actualizers are skilled in operationalizing and technologizing the achievement of goals. Non-actualizers are unable to go beyond developing vague concepts in any area of endeavor.

The case studies are interesting in terms of seeing the data translated into live people (Chapter 8). These actualizers are characterized by their creativity and productivity in both processing data and producing products. Perhaps most important, they have persevered over their lifetimes—in the face of all obstacles and crises—to continue to actualize their potential. Other than that and their skills, they began as we did. Only they chose to be more. And paid the price for being more. And, they say it is worth it!

At any given point in time, we are either living or dying (Chapter 9). The elusive plateau that we all seek throughout our lives—in privatizing our motives or preparing in our youth for retirement— are in reality dangerous precipices. There is no middle ground—no middle age—no neutral zone. We are either young or old—alive or dead! The great irony is that most people are afraid of the implications of the life choice. They do not want to be isolated and ostracized. For some perverse reason, they are not afraid of the implications of the death choice. If they were, they would realize at the first compromise of their integrity, at the first surrender of their selfhood, they already know how they are going to die—in agony.

Clearly, it is not possible to actualize human potential while becoming more restrictive in the variability of our human dimensions (Chapter 10). It is only possible to actualize our human potential by expanding our human dimensions and moving towards qualitatively higher and absolutely healthier levels of functioning. We simply must be achieving greater numbers and higher levels of responses in physical fitness, emotional responsiveness, and intellectual initiative. These levels are observable and measurable. They tell us whether we are living or dying.

The human being is like a multidimensional model (Chapter 11): There is the learning or actualization process in which he or she engages; there are the skills he or she learns; there are the resources he or she actualizes. All of these dimensions interact and the effects of these interactions are cumulative. In addition, the human being can incorporate in his or her make-up dimensions that exist in space outside of the individual. In other words, the human being is the analogue of life's dimensions. In one respect, those dimensions of the world exist only as extensions of the human brain. In another respect, those dimensions have a reality of their own that can be incorporated into the human brain. The human brain is as multidimensional as is his or her world. The world is as multi-dimensional as is the human brain. The human brain and the world in which it exists are one and the same.

The most fundamental set of skills the actualized person possesses is learning skills (Chapter 12). These skills are not the ap-parency of intellectualism. They are not the games people play to project an image of inquisitiveness (My friend, Jim Drasgow, always used to say that the essence of graduate training was to learn to ask a seemingly astute question at a colloquium). Learning skills reflect a continuously open system that processes input and focuses output. With it go responsibilities for maintaining the system as open and sharp. When the systems of fully functioning people are open, they process input and offer totally new perspectives, dimensions, and initiatives than those with which they or others began. When individuals allow their energies to be depleted and their systems to close down, they are at best temporarily static in reflecting a fixed and uni-dimensional and unilateral position. At worst, they are the destructive critics who cannot tolerate the excellence that, alas, only yesterday they may have striven for.

$E = P \cdot E^2 \cdot I^3$

We began our text with a reformulation of Einstein's equation for physical energy: $E = mc^2$. We defined the E in terms of human energy or human effectiveness or our effectiveness in actualizing our human potential. We defined the m in terms of the individual's motivation to actualize his or her potential. Finally, we defined the c in terms of the individual's competencies in their substantive specialties and demonstrated its power relative to m by squaring it. We would like to elaborate now upon this formula and give its terms a more precise meaning and weight. The formula we are developing is again the formula for human energy or effectiveness in actualizing our human potential.

$E =$

The achievement of E means that, within one's constitutional limits, a person is going to become his or her ideal. An actualized person is going to converge his or her fully developed resources—

physical, emotional and intellectual—upon the experience at hand while simultaneously being aware of the succession of experiences that will follow. In other words, the actualized person is going to be able to describe, predict, and ultimately create his or her world. Of course, the ideal is always changing in relation to the maturity of one's developmental experience. Where a person wants to be becomes where he or she is once there.

What actualization means practically for an individual is that he or she can do all the things he or she wants or needs to do in life. The actualized individual will have the physical energy to function with intensity and stamina on the tasks before him or her. The fully functioning person will have the necessary personal and interpersonal motivation to be sustained over a lifetime of hurdles enroute to achieving his or her essential mission. The person who realizes his or her full potential will emphasize intellectual achievement in specialty skill development as well as the interactive learning and teaching process that makes such specialty skill development possible. Let us take a deeper look at how these dimensions interact.

The physical factor is a facilitative but insufficient condition of actualizing human potential. It energizes the actualization process. As such, its contribution is significant but limited relative to the other factors.

$E = P$

The emotional factor is really two factors—the intrapersonal and the interpersonal motivation. The former taps a person's commitment outside of himself or herself. The latter taps a person's commitment to the commitments of others. If we collapse E' and E'' and square the result, we complement the actualization formula with the appropriate power for E.

$E = P \cdot E^2$

Finally, the intellectual factor is really three factors: substance, learning, and teaching. Substance represents the individual's unique contribution. Learning represents the individual's ability to grow in contribution. Teaching represents the individual's ability to communicate to others and thus receive the requisite feedback for further learning. If we collapse I', I", and I'", and cube them, we represent the dominating power of the intellect in an equation for actualizing human potential.

$$E = P \cdot E^2 \cdot I^3$$

This formula is in effect a reformulation of the human translation of $E = mc^2$. The physical factor is added but limited. It is a necessary but insufficient condition for most purposes outside of athletic prowess. The emotional factor is expanded and squared to account for its catalytic force in generating the actualization process. The intellectual factor is expanded further and cubed to accommodate its overwhelming predominancy in developing human potential.

In a very real sense, actualizing human potential is like a multi-staged rocket. There are at least three stages: The physical stage provides the necessary energy for the efforts and is deemphasized; the emotional stage provides the necessary motivation for the efforts and is deemphasized; the intellectual stage takes over and manages the effort thereafter. These stages may be recycled over and over again—the physical stage being expanded to energize still greater efforts, the emotional stage being expanded to motivate greater efforts, and the intellectual stage being expanded to manage greater efforts.

Once we have provided the base of physical energy and mobilized the effort with emotivation, the remainder is intellectual. The physical provides a base from which we move. The emotional serves to create and expand the directions in which we move. The intellectual represents how and how well we move. The intellectual factors represent our essential contributions to our worlds and ourselves.

The formula for human effectiveness can be applied in absolute or relative terms. Absolute standards for the various levels of functioning may be developed for the purposes of comparison between individuals. Simply stated, some people are sick and others healthy in absolute terms of a variety of criteria. Indeed, without the extremes—especially the ideals for health—we would not know what was possible. We would never know the extent of our physical energy resources. We would never know the depths to which our personal commitments and love relationships could go. We would never go places where we had never been because our minds could not leap before us.

On the other hand, for the individual the formula can be employed most meaningfully in a relative sense for one's own purposes.

In other words, the only real comparison he or she makes is with himself or herself. Thus, the individual can employ the formula like a favorability or satisfaction scale—determining what would be the most favorable levels of functioning within or between areas; diagnosing where he or she is relative to that ideal; developing the levels of achievement through which he or she must pass to achieve the ideal.

TOWARD MEANINGFUL QUANTIFICATION

It is in the nature of research and development in the area of human resource development to employ scales that relate to the criteria of meaning. That is to say, these scales meaningfully describe functional differences in the development of human resources. Between Levels 2 and 3, for example, we find the differences between survival and adaptability in health; incentives and pride in personal emotivation; attending and responding in interpersonal emotivation; concepts and principles in substance; involving and exploring in learning; or developing content and diagnosing in teaching. The levels describe meaningful differences in human functionality.

There are several levels of assumptions involved in developing these scales. The first is the random assumption: A randomly selected number of people on any criteria will yield random results. That is, there will be no functional differences. Of course, if the N (number of people) selected is large enough, the differences between groups may be statistically significant. But these differences are meaningless in terms of human functionality because, in the everyday world many people are functioning within the very limited range between being detractors and observers—between surviving and being sick physically, emotionally, and intellectually.

Related to this assumption is the training assumption: One gets what he or she trains or teaches for. To expect serendipitous generalizations or transfers from teaching A to outcome B is not rational, even though the proponents of rigor carry precisely this research strategy out reductio ad absurdum. They insist that the outcome measures be independent of the training process. Rather, in a sane system, one must train for A and test for A.

To make the training assumption, a person must have a deductive assumption: He or she must have a deductive model built inductively from generalizations based on stable bodies of phenomena and refined deductively by critical hypothesis testing in the real world. In other words, the individual must have a vision of the "ideal"—a vision of what can be and, more important, what can impact or make a difference in the real world.

My vision is a simple one: The factors that will enable each of us to actualize our human potential and to help others to actualize theirs are stamina in physical energy, a clear mission in personal emotivation, initiative in interpersonal emotivation, skill steps in substance, action strategies in learning, individualized programs in teaching. All of these characteristics represent the culmination levels of cumulative scales measuring human performance. Together, they provide an experience that is more than the sum of the parts—the courage and ability to operationalize what we do not now know.

For our purposes, quantification of the equation for actualizing human potential is a very tricky process. Since our concern is for human meaning, we cannot be restricted by criteria of rigor delivered from statistical and testing theory. Preoccupation with rigor stultifies concern for our formula and scale content by confusing the question of whether our measurements are meaningful with the questions of what they mean in scaling type and mathematical and statistical terms.

Accordingly, we will proceed to perform the mathematical operations of multiplying and empowering (squaring and cubing) our rating levels in terms that meet the criteria of human relevance. Let us begin by looking at the range of extremes that the formula is meant to portray.

If people are functioning at the lowest levels of all physical, emotional, and intellectual components—as are many people— then they have done nothing to actualize their human potential. Physically, they are sick. Emotionally, they are directionless and unattentive to others. Intellectually, they are aware only of the facts of their existence; they do not engage in learning or teaching. Indeed, it is as if they were not alive. They are Detractors. We can represent this disastrously low level of functioning by inserting Level 1 functioning in our formula as follows:

$$E = P \cdot E^2 \cdot I^3$$
$$E = 1 \cdot 1 \cdot 1 \cdot 1 \cdot 1 \cdot 1$$
$$E = 1$$

As can be seen, these people are very limited in functioning. They have no real ability to survive physically. They do not attend to incentives or other people emotivationally. They do not develop their conceptual, learning, or teaching powers to any degree. Indeed, we may conceive of them as having single and often deadly responses: At best, each has a single response that has only random application; at worst, each is a passively destructive person who is committed only to dying and taking as many people along as possible.

Let us now contrast these severely limited—indeed physically, emotionally, and intellectually retarded—people with those who have actualized their human potential. They function with stamina physically, a sense of mission and initiative emotionally, and skill steps for acting upon and individualizing programs intellectually. They are Leaders. Using the same formula for effectiveness, we can calculate their power relative to others by inserting Level 5 functioning in our formula as follows:

$$E = P \cdot E^2 \cdot I^3$$
$$E = 5 \cdot 5 \cdot 5 \cdot 5 \cdot 5 \cdot 5$$
$$E = 15{,}625$$

As can be seen, these fully functioning people are almost infinitely more powerful than their limited counterparts. Again, if we conceive of each scale as cumulative with regard to the skills involved, we may contrast people with potentially more than 15,000 responses in their repertoires with people with only one response. In any event, the numbers represent the powerful difference between most people and those few who have actualized their potential. The former are physical, emotional, and intellectual slaves. The latter are free to become who they would become.

In between these extremes lies a whole range of degrees, each more powerful than the lowest level but none even coming close to approximating the highest level of actualization. For example, people struggling as Observers (Level 2) are surviving physically; motivated by incentives and attentive to others emotionally; they develop concepts in their content and involve themselves minimally in learning and teaching their content. We can calculate their effectiveness as follows:

$$E = P \cdot E^2 \cdot I^3$$
$$E = 2 \cdot 2 \cdot 2 \cdot 2 \cdot 2 \cdot 2$$
$$E = 64$$

As can be seen, their power is relatively greater than that of people functioning at the lowest levels. Nonetheless, it is dwarfed by the power of people functioning at the highest levels. These people have no notions of being able to adapt physically, have pride in their efforts and responsiveness to others emotionally, have principles and exploring and diagnosing skills intellectually.

Similarly, people functioning at minimally effective levels as Participants have severe limitations. Such people have physical energy sufficient to adapt to the daily conditions of life, can function with pride emotivationally, are responsive to others interpersonally, can organize facts and concepts into principles substantively, are good explorers of the conditions of learning, are more than adequate for diagnosing the skills and knowledge of others in teaching. The effectiveness of such people, doing their delicate balancing act at Level 3—lingering between survival and growth—can be calculated as follows:

$$E = P \cdot E^2 \cdot I^3$$
$$E = 3 \cdot 3 \cdot 3 \cdot 3 \cdot 3 \cdot 3$$
$$E = 729$$

Clearly, such people have substantial power relative to those at lower levels. Indeed, it is a source of their price that they are better than the others. Unfortunately, such Participants usually pour all of their vital energies into maintaining their positions relative to others rather than committing themselves to growth. The Participants, whatever glimpse they have of life and leadership roles they are assigned in the Apparent World, never enter the actualization process. Consequently, while they can adapt physically, they never live with intensity; while they function with pride, they can never identify with the instrument of a mission; while they can respond to the experiences of others, they cannot personalize their problems and goals; while they can develop principles, they cannot transform them into skill objectives; while they can explore, they can never understand; while they can diagnose, they can never set goals. In short, while they do not die, they never ever really live.

On the other hand, people functioning at additive or initiative levels have begun to cross the Growing Line (Level 3). Such Contributors live with intensity physically; identify motivationally at least with the instrument of a mission; personalize experiences for others; operationalize goals substantively; understand where they are going in learning; and are able to set goals for others in teaching. Such people are engaged in growing and their effectiveness in actualizing their potential is calculated as follows:

$$E = P \cdot E^2 \cdot I^3$$
$$E = 4 \cdot 4 \cdot 4 \cdot 4 \cdot 4 \cdot 4$$
$$E = 4,096$$

The numbers represent the power of growing. These people personify the direction of growth—toward stamina, mission identification, initiative interpersonal relationships, skill steps and action learning, and individualized programs. In short, whether they falter or not, the Contributors have had an experience of the possible.

Of course, most people do not fit nicely into one consistent, across-the-board, modal level of functioning. Typically, they are relatively higher in one area than the others. Most people get their sense of identification out of specializing in one area or another. Thus, we hear the various calls of the not-so-wild: "I motivate people." "I relate." "I know my stuff." "I'm a learner." "I'm a teacher."

Unfortunately for them—even in their specialization areas—while they may function relatively higher than the other specializers, these survivors never function at levels higher than the lowest levels of the Growers. We may calculate a simple example of a typical Survivor as follows:

$$E = P \cdot E^2 \cdot I^3$$
$$P \cdot E' \quad E'' \quad I' \quad I'' \quad I'''$$
$$E = 3 \cdot 2 \cdot 2 \cdot 1 \cdot 2 \cdot 2$$
$$E = 48$$

As can be seen, such a profile yields an effectiveness score that is relatively more powerful than the lowest level functioning people. However, while these Survivors may function relatively higher than the other specializers, even in their area of specialization they typically never function at levels higher than the lowest levels of Growers. Thus, for example, while people may be attentive interpersonally, they, in their entire lifetimes, may never make a response that is accurately interchangeable with the feeling and the meaning expressed by another person. In contrast, a highly effective person, while always initiative, will always make interchangeable responses to check out the accuracy of their responses with other people.

There are other conditions that modify the power of effectiveness. For example, a person may be physically, emotionally, or intellectually handicapped. Obviously, this handicap might cap his or her development in absolute terms. However, relative to the individual, the equation may be employed to calculate effectiveness in actualizing human potential. Let us illustrate by using the example of an individual with a progressively deteriorating physical condition who has compensated by internalizing a life mission emotivationally and operationalizing it intellectually. Such a person's effectiveness may be calculated as follows:

$$E = P \cdot E^2 \cdot I^3$$
$$P \cdot E' \quad E'' \quad I' \quad I'' \quad I'''$$
$$E = 1 \cdot 5 \cdot 4 \cdot 5 \cdot 5 \cdot 5$$
$$E = 2,500$$

Such a person can demonstrate great effectiveness in actualizing human potential in spite of a debilitating handicap. Excluding these kinds of exceptions, however, people in general do not function in any one of the actualization dimensions more than one level away from the modal level of functioning. In addition, depending upon whether the person is growing or deteriorating, a discrepant level of functioning will tend to have a positive or a negative pull upon the other dimensions. Thus, a person's elevation in interpersonal skills may serve to impact all of the other P, E, and I factors positively. Similarly, the deterioration in physical fitness will impact all of the other factors negatively.

If we return again to our image of the multi-staged rocket, we can see the functions of the different factors. The physical factors lay the base or set the stage. The emotional factors mobilize the effort. The intellectual factors constitute the effort. All of these factors are recycled in expanding the base, the mobilization, and the effort.

The power of the intellect in the actualization of human potential can be seen most clearly in the quantification of the dimensions. Our humanity is our intellect. The physical and emotional factors are merely supports to energize and mobilize our use of our intellect.

IMPLICATIONS

How, then, do fully functioning or actualized people live? They are fully vital every moment—as if each were their last. They are fully committed to missions outside of themselves, thus gauging every move in terms of their overriding values. They experience with immediacy the subtle and changing nuances of feeling and meaning that occur within themselves and in others who matter to them and share these experiences with people functioning or attempting to function fully in their worlds. They give meaning to everything they do and to all who exist around them. They teach fully all that they know—holding nothing back—so that they can learn what they do not know. Always free and unencumbered by role or expectations to make choices—and always making the life choice.

How does everyone else live? As neutralized and compromised caricatures of life, they call on their depleted energy resources to convey the appearance that they are more lifeful than their neighbors ("We have sex two times a week"—whether they like it or not.). They are concerned only about their own personal career implications for every mission statement made to them ("Maybe I will and maybe I won't—it depends upon its impact on my career ladder."). They relate role-to-role to increase distance rather than intimacy ("I am feeling comfortable with you."). Using their intellects as weapons rather than the tools of their fulfillment, they study each new initiator to imitate his or her form rather than substance ("That's the latest hot button."). They criticize from a closed system ("Here's the way we do it."), and feign learning only for those things already known ("Don't teach me anything I don't already know.").

Life choices, as death choices, are simply a cumulative succession of little choices to grow up or cop out. Life is found in an increasing quantity and quality of responsibilities to grow and to help others to grow. Death is found in the various and sundry rights, rewards, and privileges people demand for their very existence—let alone their inadequate performance. Pathology leading to the death of the soul is simply the avoidance of responsibilities. Sickness is a choice just as life is a choice.

In the end, we will know the actualizers by their lifeful characteristics. Reduced to its essential ingredients, actualization means that the people have available to them the means to personalize, operationalize, and achieve any goal of human significance. Their potency comes from their skills. Reduced, non-actualization means that the people do not have available to them any means to develop, describe, and achieve any goal in any area of human endeavor. Their impotency comes from their lack of skills.

Einstein was also concerned with reversing the relationships in his equation. In so doing, he concluded that for the mass (M) increase to be measurable, the change of energy (E) per mass unit must be enormously large. He then introduced us to the terms that have become very familiar in our modern atomic world: radioactive disintegration. Schematically, the process is as follows: An atom of the mass, M, split into two atoms of the mass, M' and M'', which separate with tremendous kinetic energy. If we can imagine these two masses as brought to rest, then together they constitute somewhat less energy than was the original atom—in contradiction of the old principle of the conservation of mass.

Einstein indicated that, while we could not actually weigh the atoms individually, there were indirect methods for measuring them. In addition, he postulated the kinetic energies that are transferred to the disintegration products, M' and M''. Thus, it became possible to test and confirm the equivalence formula and to calculate in advance—from precisely determined atom weights—just how much energy will be released with any atom disintegration.

What takes place can be illustrated with the help of our rich man. The atom M is a rich miser who, during his life, gives away no money (energy). But in his will, he bequeaths his fortune to his sons M' and M'', on the condition that they give to the community a small amount, less than one thousandth of the whole estate (energy or mass). The sons together have somewhat less than the father had (the mass sum M' and M'' is somewhat smaller than the mass M of the radioactive atom). But the part given to the community, though relatively small, is still so enormously large (considered as kinetic energy) that it brings with it a great threat of evil. Averting that threat has become the most urgent problem of our time (Einstein, 1956, p. 53).

We are at the same stage of development in understanding the actualization of human potential that Einstein was when he discovered the laws of physical energy. We are also, unfortunately, at the same stage of understanding the disintegration of humanity—with or without the bomb, for the bomb is only the culminating symbol of what humans have done to themselves. The choice is ours. We can fulfill our human destiny by actualizing our human potential or cause the disintegration of humanity by failing to energize and motivate ourselves to use our intellects. By choosing to actualize our potential we show the courage to enter the unknown—confident in our ability to operationalize any goals and achieve them in successive approximations of the truth.

REFERENCES

Carkhuff, R. R. *Helping and Human Relations. Vols. I and II.* New York: Holt, Rinehart and Winston, 1969.

Einstein, A. *Out of My Later Years.* Seacaucus, N.J.: Citadel Press, 1956.

Index